SOUTH EAST
Regional R...

G000274987

CONTENTS

Key to Map Pages............ 2-3
Road Maps......................4-49
Town Plans, Airport & Port Plans...50-60
Index to Towns and Villages..........61-72

REFERENCE

MOTORWAY	**M2**
Under Construction	
Proposed	
MOTORWAY JUNCTIONS WITH NUMBERS	
Unlimited interchange **6** Limited interchange **7**	
MOTORWAY SERVICE AREA (with fuel station)	**MEDWAY** Ⓢ
with access from one carriageway only	Ⓢ
MAJOR ROAD SERVICE AREAS (with fuel station)	**PEASE POTTAGE**
with 24 hour Facilities	Ⓢ
PRIMARY ROUTE _ (with junction number)	**58** **A14**
PRIMARY ROUTE DESTINATION	**DOVER**
DUAL CARRIAGEWAYS (A & B Roads)	
CLASS A ROAD	**A260**
CLASS B ROAD	**B2011**
MAJOR ROADS UNDER CONSTRUCTION	
MAJOR ROADS PROPOSED	
SAFETY CAMERAS WITH SPEED LIMITS	
Single Camera	30
Multiple Cameras located along road	50
Single & Multiple Variable Speed Cameras	
FUEL STATION	
GRADIENT 1:5 (20%) & STEEPER (Ascent in direction of arrow)	«
TOLL	*TOLL*
MILEAGE BETWEEN MARKERS	8
RAILWAY AND STATION	
LEVEL CROSSING AND TUNNEL	
RIVER OR CANAL	
COUNTY OR UNITARY AUTHORITY BOUNDARY	
NATIONAL BOUNDARY	+
BUILT-UP AREA	
VILLAGE OR HAMLET	o
WOODED AREA	
SPOT HEIGHT IN FEET	• 813
RELIEF ABOVE 400' (122M)	
NATIONAL GRID REFERENCE (Kilometres)	200
AREA COVERED BY TOWN PLAN	**SEE PAGE 50**

TOURIST INFORMATION

AIRPORT	✈
AIRFIELD	+
HELIPORT	⊞
BATTLE SITE AND DATE	⚔ *1066*
CASTLE (Open to Public)	⛫
CASTLE WITH GARDEN (Open to Public)	
CATHEDRAL, ABBEY, CHURCH, FRIARY, PRIORY	✝
COUNTRY PARK	
FERRY (Vehicular)	⛴
(Foot only)	
GARDEN (Open to Public)	❋
GOLF COURSE _____ 9 HOLE ___ ⛳ 18 HOLE	⛳
HISTORIC BUILDING (Open to Public)	⊞
HISTORIC BUILDING WITH GARDEN (Open to Public)	⊞
HORSE RACECOURSE	
LIGHTHOUSE	⛿
MOTOR RACING CIRCUIT	
MUSEUM, ART GALLERY	▣
NATIONAL PARK	
NATIONAL TRUST PROPERTY (Open)	*NT*
(Restricted Opening)	*NT*
NATURE RESERVE OR BIRD SANCTUARY	
NATURE TRAIL OR FOREST WALK	
PLACE OF INTEREST _____ *Monument*	•
PICNIC SITE	
RAILWAY, STEAM OR NARROW GAUGE	
THEME PARK	
TOURIST INFORMATION CENTRE	
VIEWPOINT ____ 360 degrees	
180 degrees	
VISITOR INFORMATION CENTRE	Ⓥ
WILDLIFE PARK	
WINDMILL	
ZOO OR SAFARI PARK	

SCALE

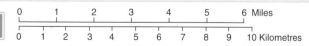

0   1   2   3   4   5   6 Miles
0 1 2 3 4 5 6 7 8 9 10 Kilometres

1:158,400
2.5 Miles to 1 Inch

Geographers' A-Z Map Company Ltd
Fairfield Road, Borough Green,
Sevenoaks, Kent TN15 8PP
01732 781000 (Enquiries & Trade Sales)
01732 783422 (Retail Sales)
www.az.co.uk
Edition 13 2014
Copyright © Geographers' A-Z Map Company Ltd.

Ordnance Survey® This product includes mapping data licensed from Ordnance Survey®
with the permission of the Controller of Her Majesty's Stationery Office.
© Crown Copyright 2013. Licence Number 100017302.

Safety camera & fuel station locations supplied by
www.PocketGPSWorld.com Copyright 2013 © PocketGPSworld.com

Base Relief by Geo-Innovations, © www.geoinnovations.co.uk
The Shopmobility logo is a registered symbol of The National Federation of Shopmobility.

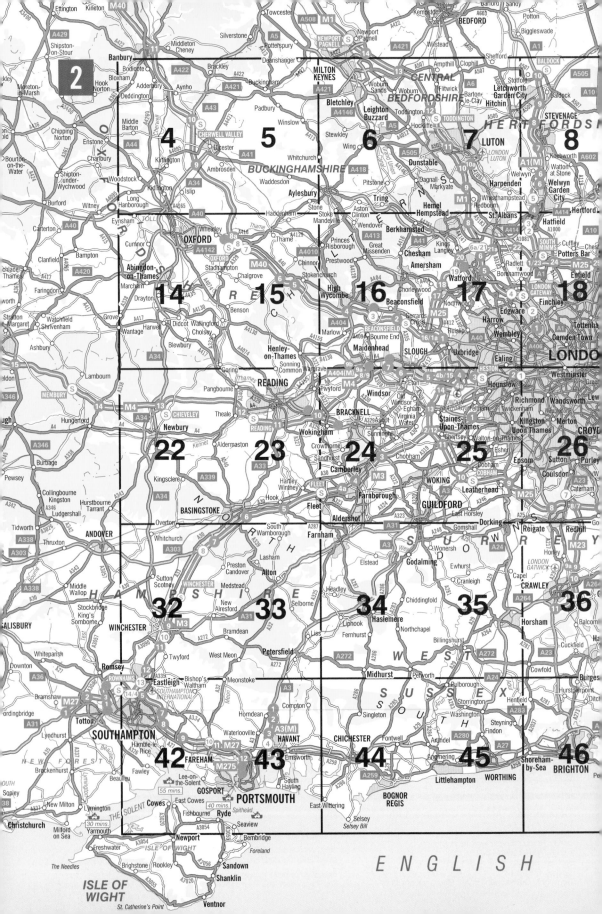

Map index grid — South-East England

Grid squares (bold numbers): 9, 10, 11, 12, 13, 19, 20, 21, 27, 28, 29, 30, 31, 37, 38, 39, 40, 41, 47, 48, 49

Major places and labels:

IPSWICH · Woodbridge · Felixstowe · Harwich · Colchester · Clacton-on-Sea · Sudbury · Braintree · Witham · Chelmsford · Maldon · Bradwell-on-Sea · Southminster · Burnham-on-Crouch · Brentwood · Basildon · SOUTHEND-ON-SEA · Canvey Island · Shoeburyness · Rayleigh · Rochford · Romford · HARLOW · Epping · Bishop's Stortford · Sawbridgeworth

Grays · Tilbury · Gravesend · Strood · ROCHESTER · CHATHAM · GILLINGHAM · Sheerness · Queenborough · ISLE OF SHEPPEY · Faversham · Whitstable · HERNE BAY · MARGATE · BROADSTAIRS · RAMSGATE · NORTH FORELAND · Dartford · Bexleyheath · Orpington · Sevenoaks · MAIDSTONE · SITTINGBOURNE · CANTERBURY · Sturry · Sandwich · DEAL · SOUTH FORELAND · DOVER · Wingham · Aylesham

TONBRIDGE · ROYAL TUNBRIDGE WELLS · Southborough · Ashford · Tenterden · Cranbrook · HYTHE · FOLKESTONE · CHANNEL TUNNEL · ROMNEY MARSH · New Romney · Littlestone-on-Sea · Greatstone-on-Sea · Lydd · DUNGENESS · Rye · Camber · Winchelsea · Rye Bay

Crowborough · Uckfield · Heathfield · Battle · Herstmonceux · Hailsham · HASTINGS · BEXHILL · EASTBOURNE · Seaford · Newhaven · Lewes · BEACHY HEAD · EAST SUSSEX

FRANCE · CAP GRIS-NEZ · BOULOGNE · STRAIT OF DOVER · Channel Tunnel

C H A N N E L

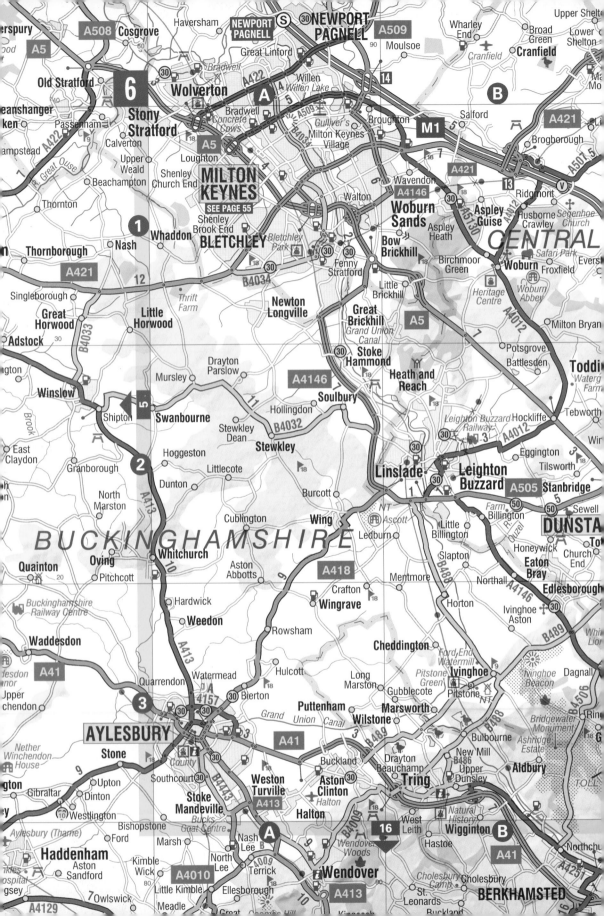

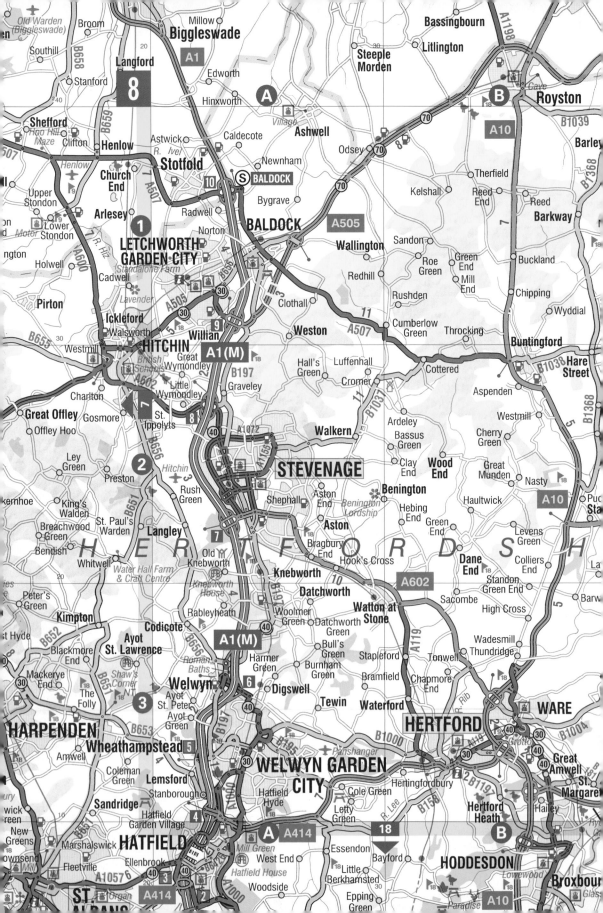

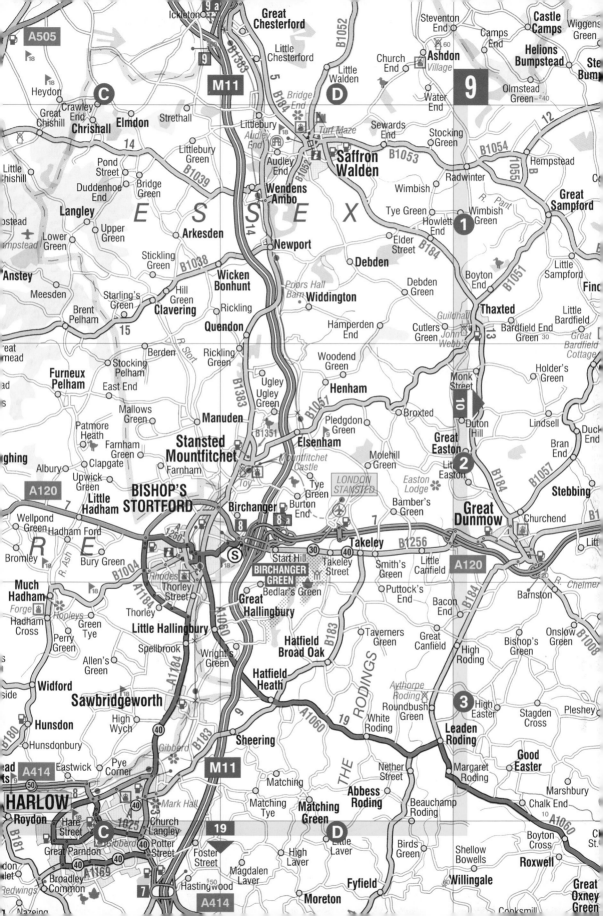

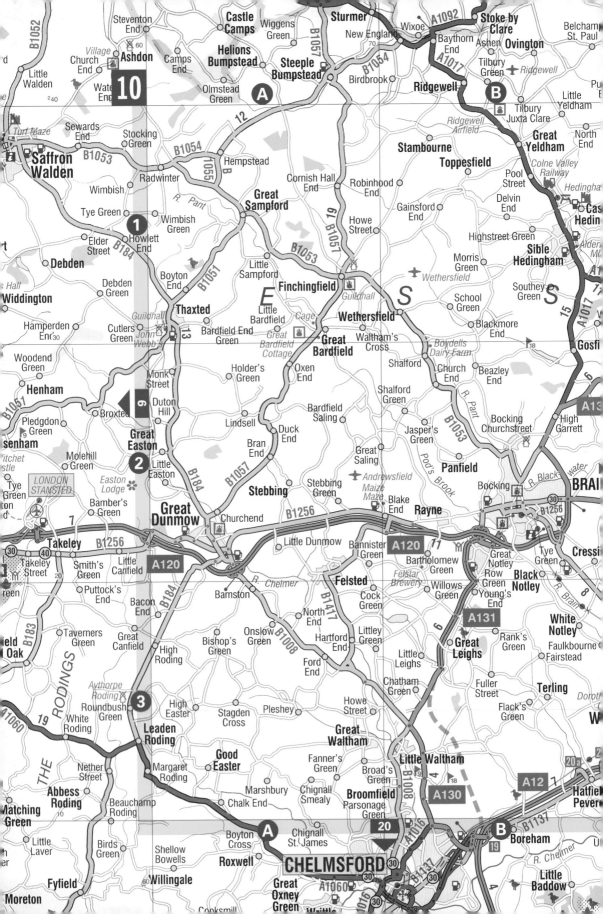

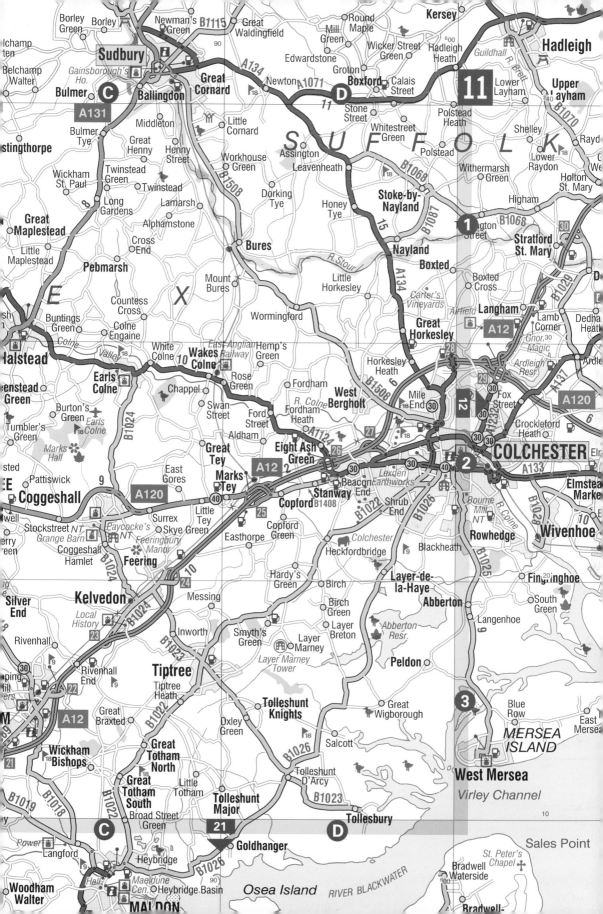

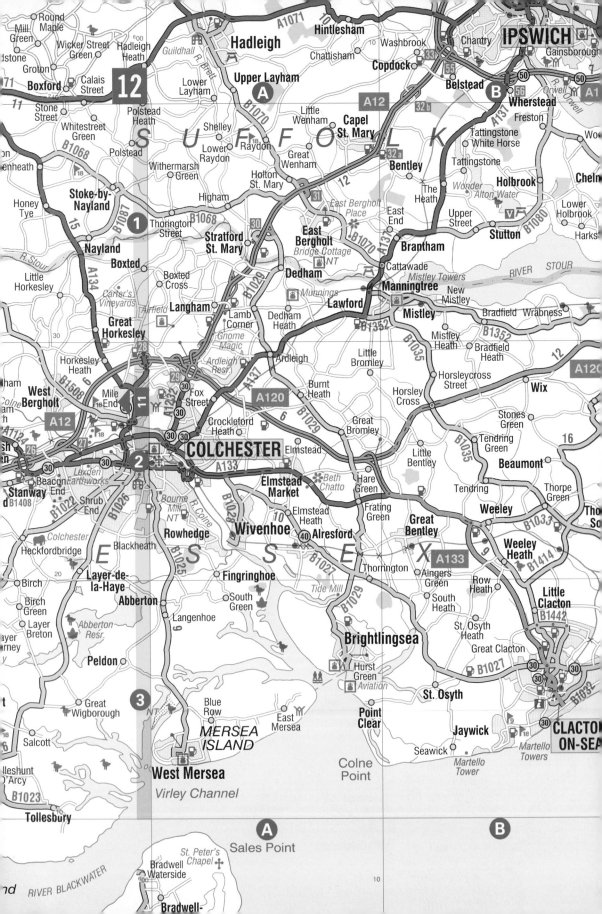

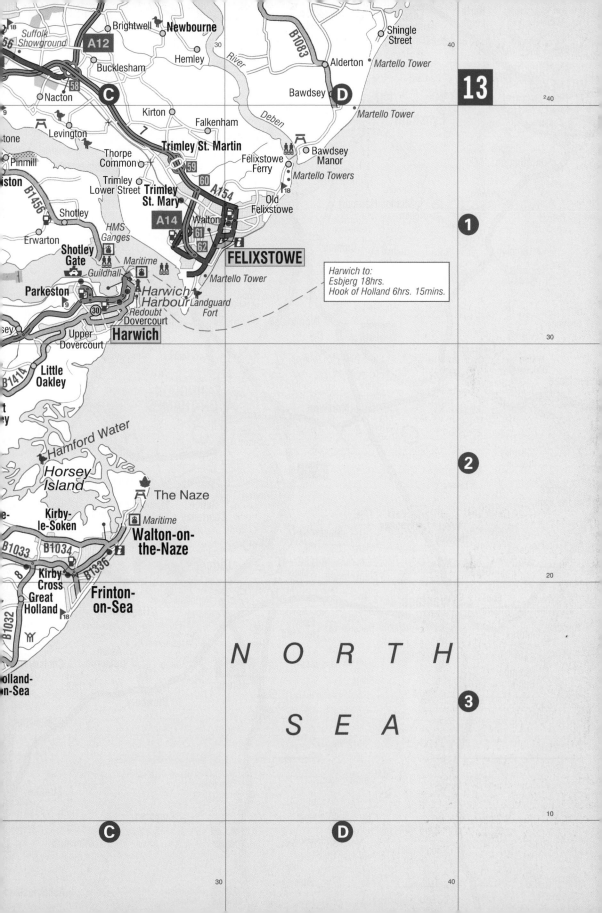

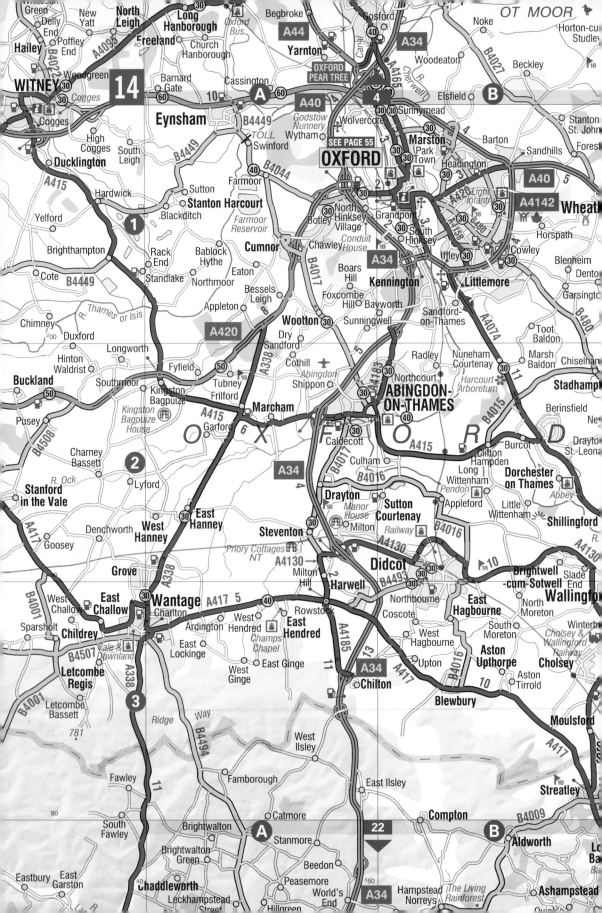

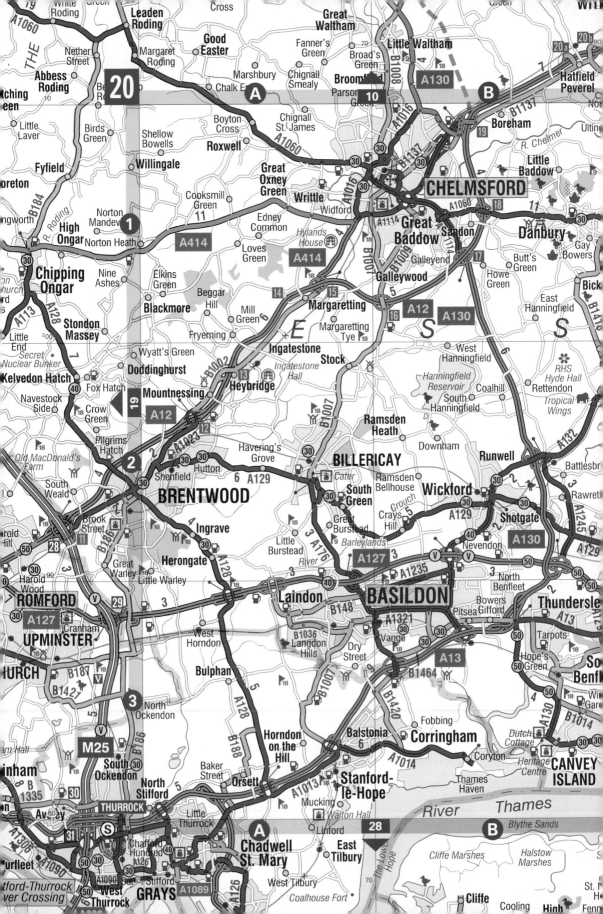

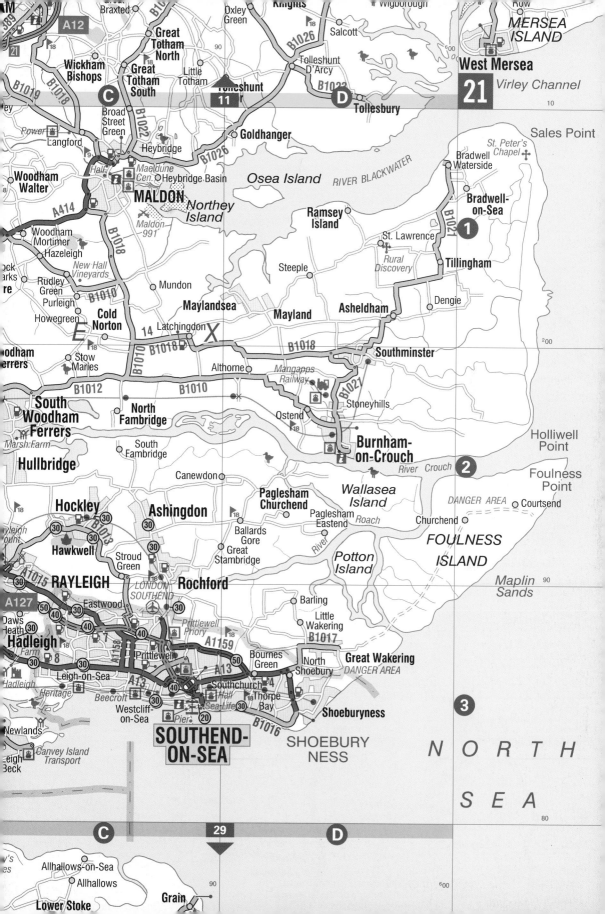

MERSEA ISLAND

West Mersea

Virley Channel

10

Sales Point

St. Peter's Chapel

Bradwell Waterside

Bradwell-on-Sea

B1027

①

St. Lawrence

Rural Discovery

Tillingham

Dengie

200

Braxted

Oxley Green

Knights

Wigborough

Row

A12

Wickham Bishops

Great Totham North

Salcott

B1026

Great Totham South

Little Totham

Tolleshunt D'Arcy

B1022

Toleshunt

C

11

D

Tollesbury

B1019

B1018

Broad Street Green

B1022

Goldhanger

Heybridge

B1026

Power

Langford

Osea Island

RIVER BLACKWATER

Woodham Walter

Maeldune Cen.

Heybridge Basin

MALDON

Northey Island

Ramsey Island

Maldon 991

A414

Woodham Mortimer

Hazeleigh

New Hall Vineyards

Steeple

B1018

Rudley Green

Purleigh

Mundon

Maylandsea

Mayland

Asheldham

Howegreen

B1010

Cold Norton

14

Latchingdon

X

Southminster

E

Stow Maries

B1018

Althorne

Mangapps Railway

Stoneyhills

B1021

B1012

B1010

B1010

Ostend

South Woodham Ferrers

North Fambridge

Marsh Farm

South Fambridge

Burnham-on-Crouch

Holliwell Point

Hullbridge

River Crouch

②

Foulness Point

Canewdon

Wallasea Island

DANGER AREA

Courtsend

Hockley

Ashingdon

Paglesham Churchend

Paglesham Eastend

Roach

Churchend

FOULNESS ISLAND

30

30

B1013

Hawkwell

30

Ballards Gore

Great Stambridge

River

Potton Island

Maplin Sands

90

RAYLEIGH

Stroud Green

Rochford

Barling

A1075

30

LONDON SOUTHEND

③

A127

Eastwood

50

40

30

Little Wakering

B1017

Daws Heath

30

40

Prittlewell Priory

A1159

Bournes Green

North Shoebury

Great Wakering

DANGER AREA

Hadleigh

Farm

8

Prittlewell

A13

Leigh-on-Sea

Heritage

Beecroft

A13

A1159

Southchurch

Thorpe Bay

Shoeburyness

Newlands

Westcliff-on-Sea

Sea Life

Pier

20

B1016

SHOEBURY NESS

N O R T H

Canvey Island Transport

Beck

SOUTHEND-ON-SEA

80

C

29

D

S E A

Allhallows-on-Sea

Allhallows

90

600

Lower Stoke

Grain

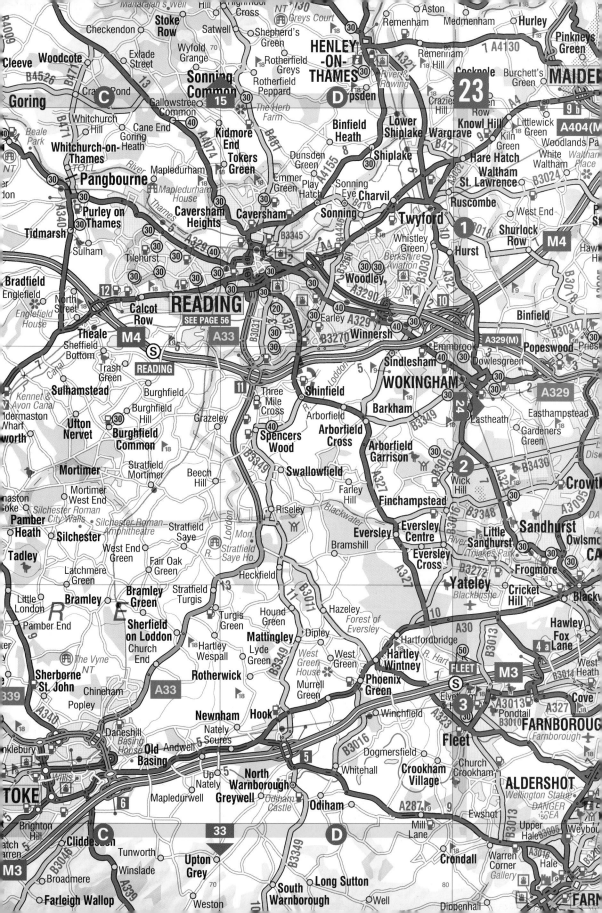

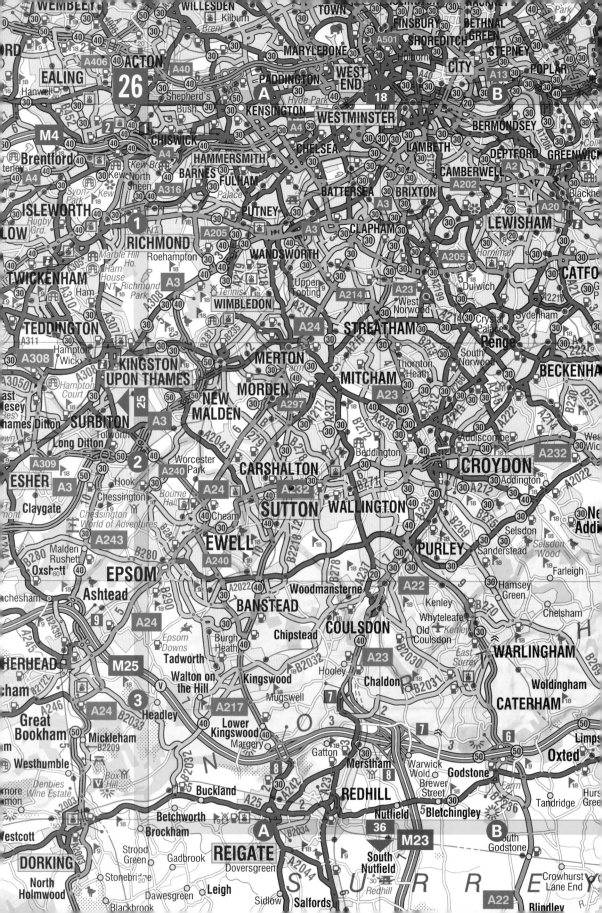

South Channel

Turner Contemporary
Walpole Bay Hotel
Lifeboat Station
Foreness Point

MARGATE
Westbrook
Cliftonville
Kingsgate

Westgate on Sea

Reculver Towers
Regulbium Roman Fort

Minnis Bay

NORTH FORELAND

Reculver
Hillborough
A299
A28
Birchington

ISLE OF THANET

St. Peter's

Westwood

Dickens House

BROADSTAIRS

oomfield
orstal
St. Nicholas at Wade

Quex House

Acol
Lydden
Spitfire & Hurricane
Northwood

Marshside
Boyden Gate
B2050
B2190

Maypole
Sarre
A299
Manston

Chislet
Monkton
Minster
KENT (MANSTON)
Tunnel

Upstreet
West Stourmouth
Plucks Gutter
R. Stour
Cliffsend
Pegwell Bay

RAMSGATE

Ramsgate to Ostend 4hrs.

Grove
East Stourmouth
Richborough Port

Stodmarsh
Westmarsh
Ware
Paramour Street
Richborough Fort
Amphitheatre
A256

Preston
Elmstone
Goldstone

Hoaden

Wickhambreaux
Wingham
Nash
Cooper Street
White

Great Stonar

Sandwich Bay

Little
Ickham
Ash
A257
Sandwich
Secret
TOLL

Bramling
Wingham
Marshborough
Woodnesborough
Guildhall

sbourne
B2046
Vineyard
Staple
Hammill
Worth

rne
Goodnestone Park
Eastry
Ham

The Small Downs

Sandown Castle

Adisham
Goodnestone
Heronden
A258

Chillenden
Knowlton
Finglesham
Betteshanger
Timeball Tower

Nonington
Northbourne
Sholden
DEAL
The Downs

ylesham
Womenswold
Frogham
Tilmanstone
Elvington
Great Mongeham
Ripple
B2056
Lifeboat Station
Walmer

Walmer

Woolage Village
Woolage Green
Bartrestone
East Kent Railway
41 East Studdal
Sutton
Ripple

Kingsdown
DANGER AREA

A260
A2
Eythorne
Shepherdswell or Sibertswold
Ashley
Ringwould

Coldred
West Langdon
Martin
Martin Mill

Wootton
A256

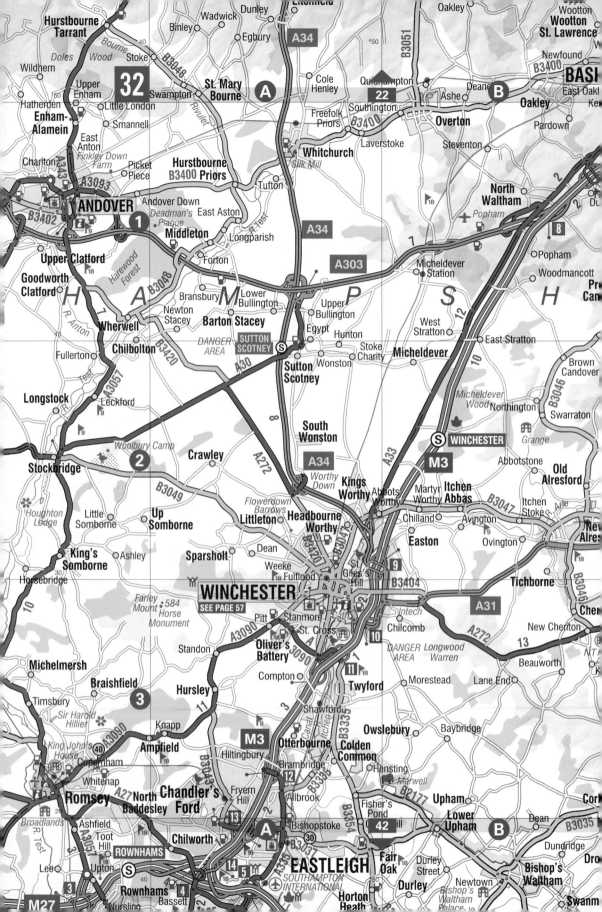

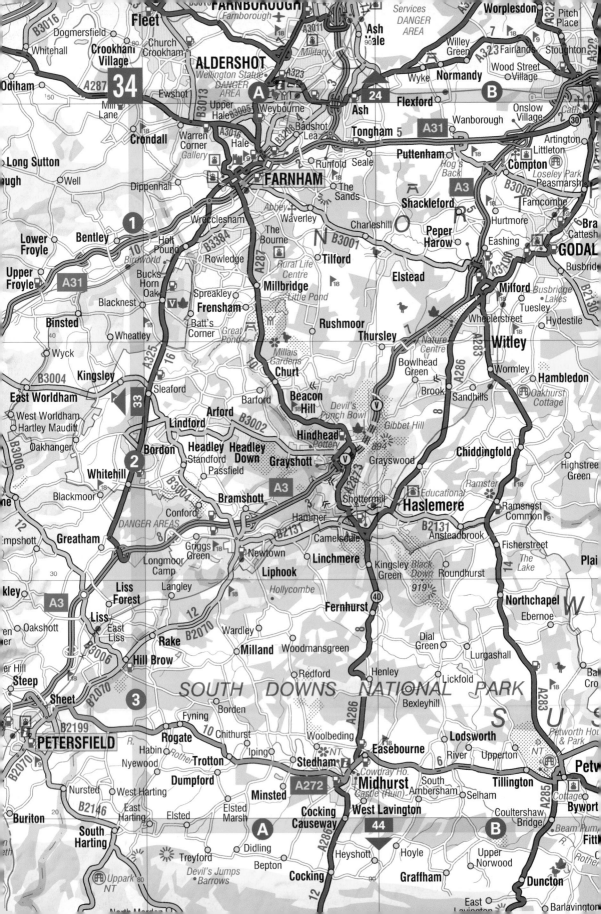

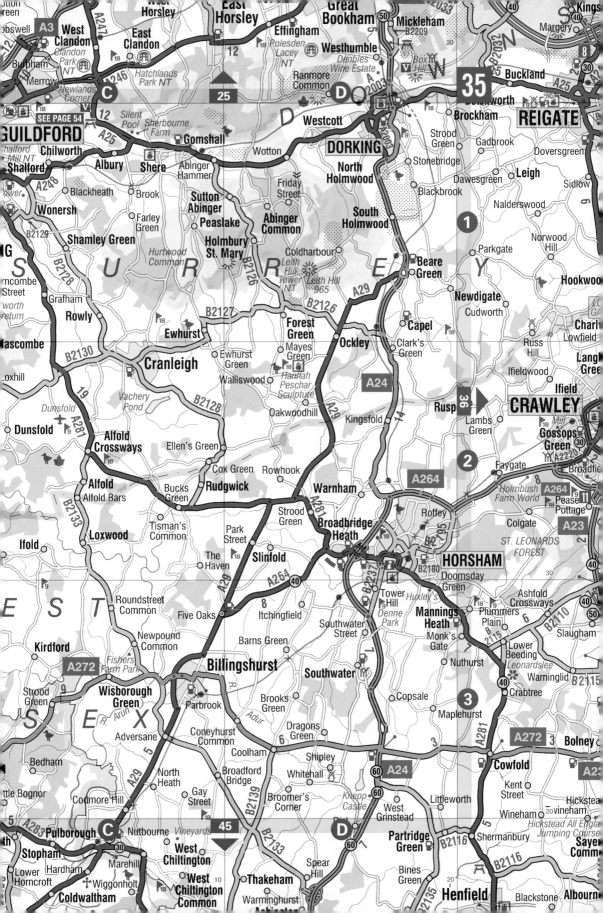

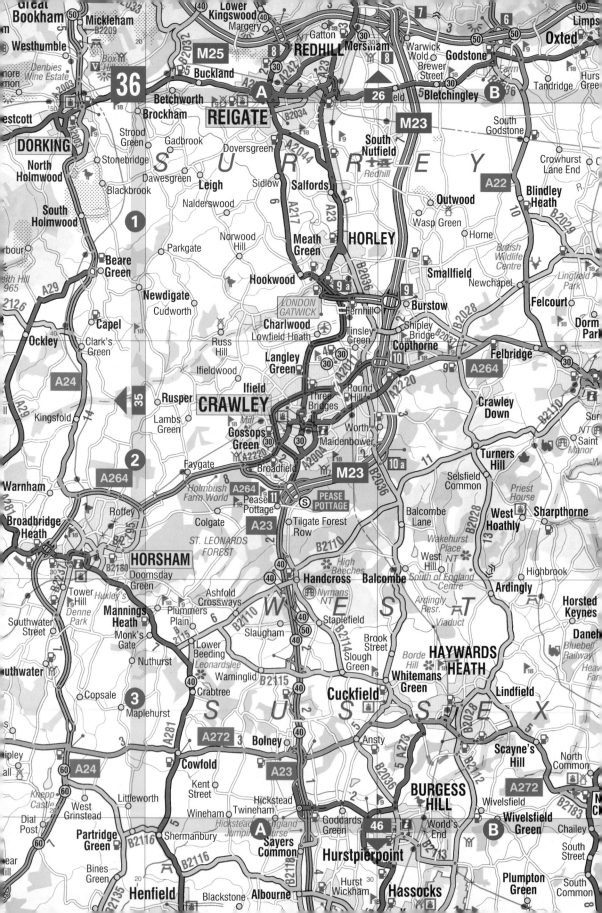

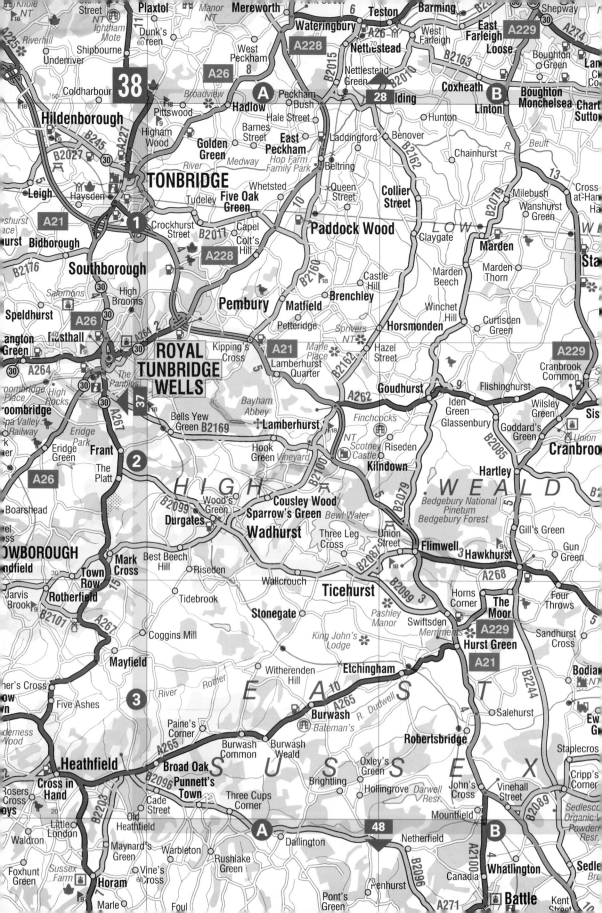

Adisham

Chillenden
Heronden
Finglesham
Betteshanger

Nonington
Knowlton

Aylesham
Northbourne
Sholden

DEAL
Timeball
Tower
40

Tilmanston
Womensw
Frogham
Elvington
31
Great Monge
Ripple
D

Lifeboat
Station
Walmer

41

The Downs

C
Woolage
Village
Bartrestone
East Kent
Railway
Eythorne
East
Studdal
Sutton

150

Woolage
Green
Shepherdswell
or Sibertswold
Ashley
Ringwould
Kingsdown

A260
Lydden
Hill
Coldred
West
Langdon
DANGER AREA

Wootton
A256
Martin
Martin Mill
Dover Patrol Monument

Lydden
Whitfield
East
Langdon
St. Margaret's at Cliffe
1

St. John's
Commandery
Temple Ewell
Kearsney
Guston
50
West
Cliffe
St. Margaret's Bay

Ewell
Minnis
A256
A2
White Cliffs NT NT
Pines

Swingfield
Street
River
Crabble
Corn Mill
Buckland
SEE PAGE 51
SOUTH FORELAND

Alkham
V
DOVER

Drellingore
Church
Hougham
Maxton
Dover to:
Calais 1hr. 30mins.
Dunkirk 2hrs.

Hawkinge
West
Hougham

Battle
Britain
Capel-le-Ferne
A20
Western Docks

13

B2011

East Wear Bay

CHANNEL TUNNEL
Folkestone to Calais 35mins.

Cheriton

gate
FOLKESTONE
SEE PAGE 56

2

STRAIT OF DOVER

30

E N G L I S H

3

C H A N N E L

20

C
D

30
40

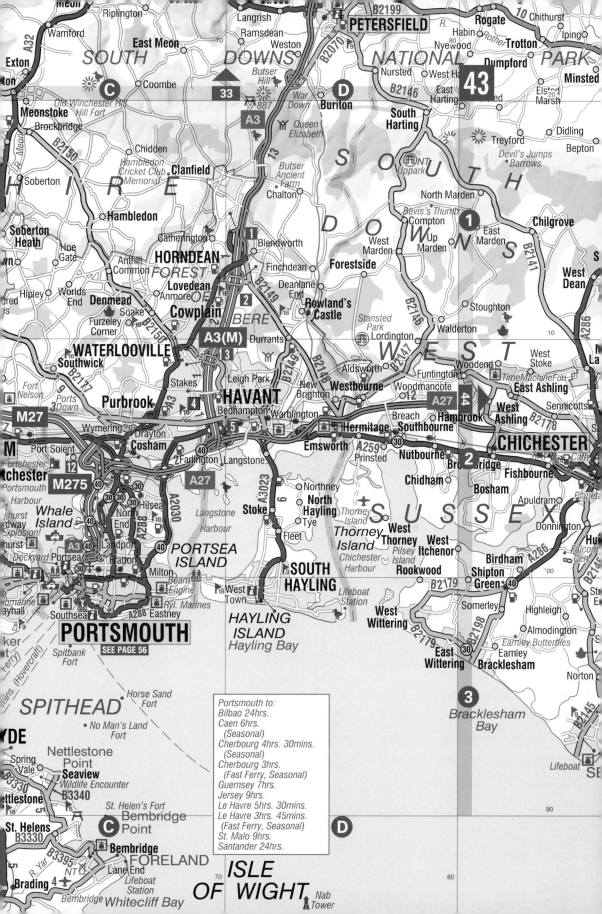

Top area (South Downs National Park):
Meon, Riplington, Langrish, **PETERSFIELD**, B2199, Rogate, 10, Chithurst, Iping, Warnford, A32, Ramsdean, Weston, Habin, Nyewood, **Trotton**, East Meon, B2070, 9, Nursted, West Ha, **Dumpford**, **Minsted**, Exton, SOUTH, DOWNS, Coombe, B2146, East Harting, Elsted Marsh, **43**, ton, Meonstoke, C, Butser Hill, War Down, **D**, **Buriton**, South Harting, Brockbridge, Old Winchester Hill Fort, 33, 887, A3, Queen Elizabeth, Treyford, Didling, B2150, Chidden, Hambledon Cricket Club Memorial, **Clanfield**, S O U T H, NT Uppark, Bepton, Soberton, Butser Ancient Farm, Chalton, North Marden, Devil's Jumps Barrows, **Hambledon**, Catherington, Blendworth, Bevis's Thumb, Compton, Up Marden, **1**, East Marden, **Chilgrove**, Soberton Heath, 13, HORNDEAN, Finchdean, West Marden, D O W N S, B2141, Hoe Gate, FOREST, Lovedean, Deanlane End, Forestside, Anthill Common, Anmore, Rowland's Castle, Stoughton, **West Dean**, Hipley, Worlds End, **Denmead**, Soake, Cowplain, OF, Stansted Park, Lordington, Walderton, 10, A286, Furzeley Corner, BERE, 18, WEST, **WATERLOOVILLE**, A3(M), Durrants, B2149, B2148, Aldsworth, B2147, Woodend, West Stoke, Southwick, 3, Woodmancote, TimeMachineFun, La, B2177, Stakes, Leigh Park, New Brighton, **Westbourne**, 12, Funtington, **East Ashling**, **Purbrook**, A3, 4, **HAVANT**, Bedhampton, Warblington, Breach, Hambrook, West Ashling, Sennicotts, M27, Fort Nelson, Ports Down, 9, Wymering, Drayton, 18, 5, Hermitage, Southbourne, B2178, M, Port Solent, Cosham, Farlington, Langstone, Emsworth, A259, Prinsted, Nutbourne, 30, **CHICHESTER**, chester, 12, M275, A2030, Northney, North Hayling, Chidham, **2**, Bro, Fishbourne, Portsmouth Harbour, A27, Stoke, Tye, SUSSEX, Bosham, Apuldram, Planet, Whale Island, North End, Langstone Harbour, Fleet, Thorney Island, West Thorney, West Itchenor, Donnington, A3, Landpor, Fratton, PORTSEA ISLAND, SOUTH HAYLING, Thorney Island, Pilsey Island, Rookwood, Birdham, Shipton Green, Hut, Falcon, Dockyard, Portsea, Milton, Beam Engine, Lifeboat Station, Chichester Harbour, B2179, 40, Southsea, A288, Eastney, Ryl. Marines, 18, West Town, HAYLING ISLAND, Hayling Bay, West Wittering, Somerley, Highleigh, Almodington, **PORTSMOUTH**, SEE PAGE 56, Spitbank Fort, B2179, B2198, Earnley Butterflies, Earnley, Norton, SPITHEAD, Horse Sand Fort, Portsmouth to:, **3**, East Wittering, Bracklesham, YDE, No Man's Land Fort, Nettlestone Point, Seaview, Bracklesham Bay, Lifeboat, Spring Vale, Wildlife Encounter, B3340, St. Helen's Fort, Bembridge Point, St. Helens, B3330, C, Bembridge, FORELAND, R. Yar, B3395, NT, Lane End, D, Brading, 4, Lifeboat Station, ISLE, OF WIGHT, Nab Tower, Bembridge, Whitecliff Bay, 70, 80, 90

Ferry times box (Portsmouth to:):
Portsmouth to:
Bilbao 24hrs.
Caen 6hrs. (Seasonal)
Cherbourg 4hrs. 30mins. (Seasonal)
Cherbourg 3hrs. (Fast Ferry, Seasonal)
Guernsey 7hrs.
Jersey 9hrs.
Le Havre 5hrs. 30mins.
Le Havre 3hrs. 45mins. (Fast Ferry, Seasonal)
St. Malo 9hrs.
Santander 24hrs.

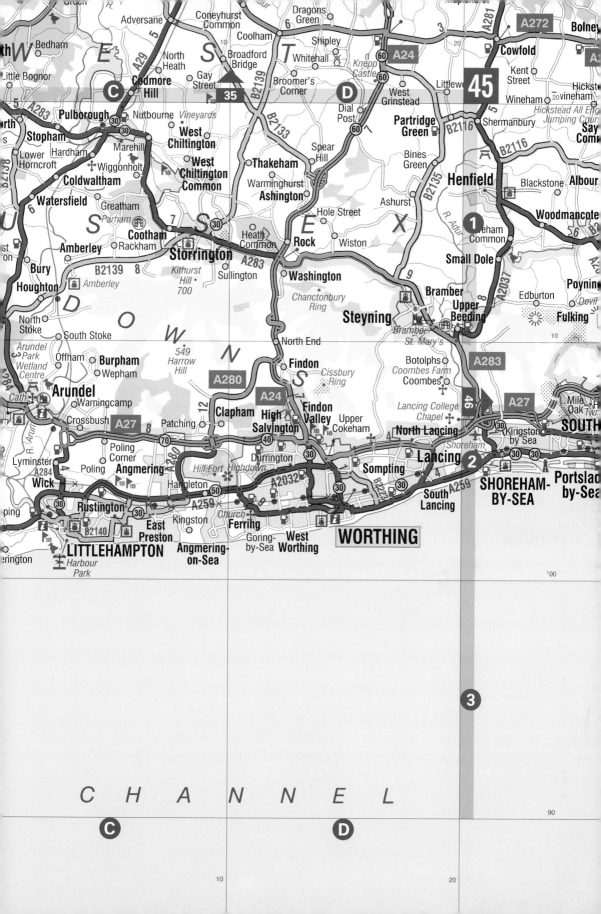

Map labels (West Sussex, England):

W · Bedham · Little Bognor · Adversane · Coneyhurst Common · Dragons Green · Bolney · A272 · Cowfold · A281

Codmore Hill · North Heath · Gay Street · Broadford Bridge · Coolham · Shipley · Whitehall · Knepp Castle · A24 · West Grinstead · Littlew · Kent Street · Wineham · Hickst · vineham · Hickstead All Eng Jumping Cour

C · A29 · B2139 · 35 · B2133 · D · 60 · 45 · Say Com

A283 · Pulborough · Nutbourne · Vineyards · Broomer's Corner · Dial Post · 60 · Partridge Green · B2116 · Shermanbury

Stopham · West Chiltington · Spear Hill · West Grinstead · Bines Green · B2135 · Henfield · Blackstone · Albour

Lower Horncroft · Hardham · Marehill · Wiggonholt · West Chiltington Common · Thakeham · Warminghurst · Ashington · Ashurst · eham Common · 1 · Woodmancote

Coldwaltham · Watersfield · Greatham · Sparham · Cootham · Rackham · Storrington · Heath Common · Rock · Wiston · Hole Street · Small Dole · A2037 · 8 · Poyning · Edburton · Devil

Amberley · B2139 · 8 · Kithurst Hill 700 · Sullington · A283 · Washington · Chanctonbury Ring · Bramber · Upper Beeding · Fulking

Bury · Amberley · Houghton · North Stoke · South Stoke · Storrington · Steyning · Bramber St. Mary's · 10

DOWNS · 549 Harrow Hill · North End · Botolphs · Coombes Farm · Coombes · A283

Arundel Park Wetland Centre · Offham · Burpham · Wepham · Cissbury Ring · Lancing College Chapel · 46 · A27 · Mile Oak · SOUTH

Arundel · Warningcamp · Cath · Crossbush · A27 · 8 · Patching · A280 · A24 · Clapham · High Salvington · Findon · Findon Valley · Upper Cokeham · North Lancing · Kingston by Sea

Lyminster · A284 · Poling Corner · Poling · Angmering · Hangleton · 50 · 70 · 40 · Durrington · 30 · Highdown Hill·Fort · Sompting · Lancing · 4 · Shoreham · 2 · SHOREHAM-BY-SEA · Portslade by-Sea

Wick · Rustington · Kingston · A259 · A2032 · 30 · South Lancing · A259 · Portslad

Littlehampton · East Preston · Angmering-on-Sea · Ferring · Goring-by-Sea · West Worthing · Church · **WORTHING**

Harbour Park · B2140 · B2139

C H A N N E L

C · D · 3

10 · 20 · 90 · 100

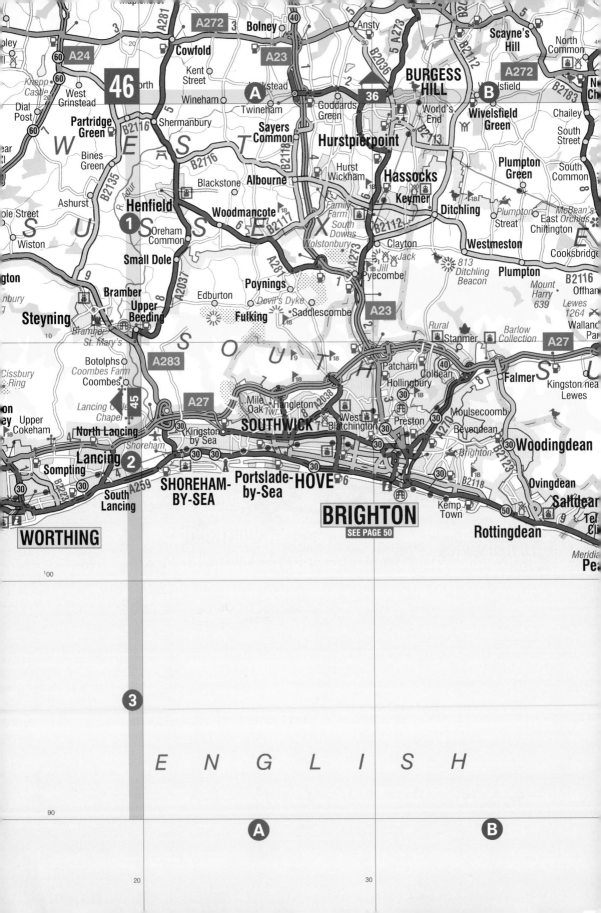

Heathfield, Cross in Hand, Rosers Cross, Waldron, Little London, Foxhunt Green, Sussex Farm, Horam, Golden Cross, Lower Dicker, Upper Dicker, Michelham Priory, Arlington, Heritage Centre, HAILSHAM, Polegate, Folkington, Wannock, Willingdon, Jevington, Willingdon Hill, East Dean, Friston, Seven Sisters Sheep Centre, Countryside Centre, BEACHY HEAD

Paine's Corner, Burwash Common, Burwash Weald, Broad Oak, Punnett's Town, Three Cups Corner, Cade Street, Heathfield, Maynard's Green, Vine's Cross, Warbleton, Rushlake Green, Marle Green, Foul Mile, Cowbeech, Stunts Green, Herstmonceux, Windmill Hill, Bodle Street Green, Magham Down, Hellingly, Horsebridge, Herstmonceux Science Centre, Observatory Science Centre, Wartling, Boreham Street, Hooe Common, Hooe, Pevensey Levels, Hankham, Courthouse, Westham, Pevensey, Pevensey Bay, Norman's Bay, Langney, Friday Street, Hampden Park, Stone Cross, Ratton Village, Old Town, EASTBOURNE, Langney Point, Fort Fun, Treasure Island, Redoubt Fortress, Lifeboat

Dallington, Brightling, Hollingrove, Mountfield, Netherfield, Penhurst, Pont's Green, Brownbread Street, Catsfield, Ninfield, Lunsford's Cross, Little Common, Cooden, BEXHILL, Sidley, Bulverhythe, St Leonards

Robertsbridge, Staplecross, Cripp's Corner, John's Cross, Vinehall Street, Whatlington, Battle, Kent Street, Abbey, Hastings 1066, Beauport Park, Telham, Henley's Down, Crowhurst, Hollington, Sedlescombe, Bateman's, Oxley's Green

Pevensey Bay

Road numbers: A265, A21, A267, A271, A269, A259, A22, A27, A2270, A2290, A2100, A2036, A2089, B2096, B2203, B2204, B2095, B2104, B2191, B2192, B2182, B2089, B2092, B2099, B2105

EAST SUSSEX

SEE PAGE 51

Zone markers: 48, 38
Grid references: A, B
Numbered circles: 1, 2, 3

Mill
Corner
Clayhill
Peasmarsh
Rye Foreign
B2082
Houghton
Green
8
WALLAND
MARSH
600
A259
Playden
Rye
East Guldeford
39
D
49
Lydd
Town
Denge
Marsh
20
B2075
Chitcombe
C
River
Tillingh
Ypres T
Camber
Jury's
Gap
DANGER AREA
Broad
Oak
B2089
Udimore
Lamb
Ho.NT
SEX
Brede
Brede
River
Camber
Rye
Harbour
Winchelsea
Lidham
Hill
Broad
Street
Rye Bay
West   Road
eam Engines
aylor
ards
12
Court
Hall
1
Icklesham
Winchelsea
Beach
A28
Westfield
Guestling
Thorn
Three Oaks
Pett
10
Guestling
Green
Baldslow
B2093
A259
Cliff End
2
21
St.
Helen's
Fairlight
Cove
Ore
Fairlight
A2707
30
ENGLISH
Blue Reef Aquarium
Shipwreck
100
30
HASTINGS
ds

CHANNEL

3

90

C   D

90   600

CITY & TOWN CENTRE PLANS

Brighton & Hove	50	Medway Towns	54	Windsor	57	London Stansted
Canterbury	51	Milton Keynes	55	London Gatwick		Airport Plan	59
Dover	51	Oxford	55	Airport Plan	58	Newhaven Port Plan	60
Eastbourne	51	Portsmouth	56	London Heathrow		Portsmouth Port Plan	60
Folkestone	56	Reading	56	Airport Plan	58	
Guildford	54	Southampton	57	London Luton		
London	52-53	Winchester	57	Airport Plan	59	

Reference to Town Plans

MOTORWAY	**M2**	ABBEY, CATHEDRAL, PRIORY ETC.	✝
MOTORWAY UNDER CONSTRUCTION		BUS STATION	
MOTORWAY JUNCTIONS WITH NUMBERS	**4** **5**	CAR PARK (Selection of)	P
Unlimited Interchange **4** Limited Interchange **5**		CHURCH	✝
PRIMARY ROUTE	**A21**	CITY WALL	
DUAL CARRIAGEWAYS		FERRY (Vehicular) (Foot only)	
CLASS A ROAD	**A260**	GOLF COURSE	
CLASS B ROAD	**B2011**	HELIPORT	
MAJOR ROADS UNDER CONSTRUCTION		HOSPITAL	H
MAJOR ROADS PROPOSED		LIGHTHOUSE	
MINOR ROADS		MARKET	
SAFETY CAMERA	30	NATIONAL TRUST PROPERTY (Open)	NT
FUEL STATION		(Restricted opening)	NT
RESTRICTED ACCESS		PARK & RIDE	P+
PEDESTRIANIZED ROAD & MAIN FOOTWAY		PLACE OF INTEREST	
ONE-WAY STREETS		POLICE STATION	▲
TOLL	TOLL	POST OFFICE	★
RAILWAY AND STATION		SHOPPING AREA (Main street and precinct)	
UNDERGROUND / METRO & D.L.R. STATION	DLR	SHOPMOBILITY	
LEVEL CROSSING AND TUNNEL		TOILET	▽
TRAM STOP AND ONE WAY TRAM STOP		TOURIST INFORMATION CENTRE	ℹ
BUILT-UP AREA		VIEWPOINT	
		VISITOR INFORMATION CENTRE	V

BRIGHTON and HOVE

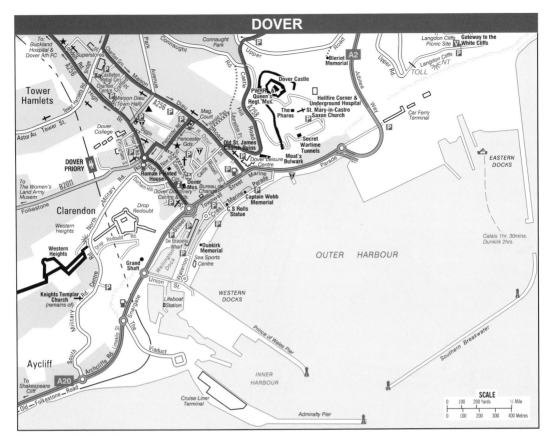

DOVER

To:
Buckland
Hospital &
Dover Ath FC

Tower
Hamlets

Astor Av.   Tower St.

Clarendon

Western
Heights

Western
Heights

Ycliff

To:
Shakespeare
Cliff

Superstores

Charlton Cen.

Castleton
Retail Cen.
Charlton
Centre

Maison Dieu
(Town Hall)

Dover
College

DOVER
PRIORY

To
The Women's
Land Army
Museum

Military Rd.

Drop
Redoubt

Drop Redoubt Rd.

Grand
Shaft

Knights Templar
Church
(remains of)

A20   Archcliffe Rd.

Old Folkestone Road

Connaught
Park

Upper Rd.

Mag.
Court

Dover Mus.

Roman Painted
House & Cln.

Old St. James
Church Ruins

Dover Discovery
Centre & Lib.

Bureau de
Change

Townwall

Cross

C S Rolls
Statue

Captain Webb
Memorial

De Bradelei
Wharf

Dunkirk
Memorial
Sea Sports
Centre

Union St.

Lifeboat
Station

Viaduct

Cruise Liner
Terminal

Bleriot
Memorial

A2

Dover Castle

PWRR &
Queen's
Regt. Mus.

The
Pharos

St. Mary-in-Castro
Saxon Church

Hellfire Corner &
Underground Hospital

Secret
Wartime
Tunnels

Moat's
Bulwark

Marine
Parade

Parade

Langdon Cliffs
Picnic Site

Gateway to the
White Cliffs

Langdon Cliffs
NT

TOLL

Car Ferry
Terminal

EASTERN
DOCKS

OUTER   HARBOUR

Calais 1hr. 30mins.
Dunkirk 2hrs.

WESTERN
DOCKS

INNER
HARBOUR

Prince of Wales Pier

Admiralty Pier

Southern Breakwater

SCALE
0   100   200 Yards   ¼ Mile
0   100   200   300   400 Metres

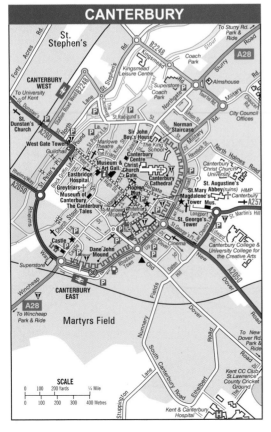

CANTERBURY

St.
Stephen's

CANTERBURY
WEST

To University
of Kent

St.
Dunstan's
Church

West Gate Towers

Guildhall

Eastbridge
Hospital

Greyfriars

Museum of
Canterbury

The Canterbury
Tales

Castle

Superstore

CANTERBURY
EAST

A28
To Wincheap
Park & Ride

Martyrs Field

To Sturry Rd.
Park &
Ride

B2248

A28

Coach
Park

Kingsmead
Leisure Centre

Superstore
Coach Park

Almshouse

City Council
Offices

Norman
Staircase

Sir John
Boy's House

Marlowe
Theatre

The Friars

Museum &
Art Gall.

Canterbury
Centre

Roman
Mus.

Dane John
Mound

The King's
School

Canterbury
Cathedral

Christ
Church
Gate

St. Augustine's

St.Mary Abbey (ruins)

Magdalene's
Tower Mus.

St. George's
Tower

Cinema

Canterbury
Christ Church
University

HMP
Canterbury

A257

St. Martin's Hill

Canterbury College &
University College
for the Creative Arts

A2050

To New
Dover Rd.
Park &
Ride

Kent CC Club
St.Lawrence
County Cricket
Ground

Kent & Canterbury
Hospital

SCALE
0   100   200 Yards   ¼ Mile
0   100   200   300   400 Metres

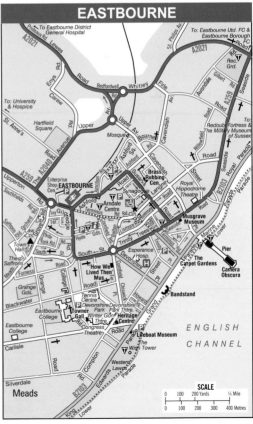

EASTBOURNE

To Eastbourne District
General Hospital

To: Eastbourne Utd. FC &
Eastbourne Borough
FC

A2021

Bedfordwell

Whitley

To: University
& Hospice

Hartfield
Square

Mosque

Rec.
Grd.

To:
Redoubt Fortress &
The Military Museum
of Sussex

St. Anne's

Upper

EASTBOURNE

Enterprise
Shop

Brass
Rubbing
Cen.

Arndale
Centre

Royal
Hippodrome
Theatre

Musgrave
Museum

Pier

The
Carpet Gardens

Camera
Obscura

Bandstand

How We
Lived Then
Mus.

The
Saffrons

Tennis
Centre

Eastbourne
College

Eastbourne
College

Devonshire
Park

Towner
Gall.

Winter Gdn.
Thtre.

Devonshire Park
Thtre.

Heritage
Centre

Congress
Theatre

Lifeboat Museum

The
Wish Tower

E N G L I S H

C H A N N E L

Meads

SCALE
0   100   200 Yards   ¼ Mile
0   100   200   300   400 Metres

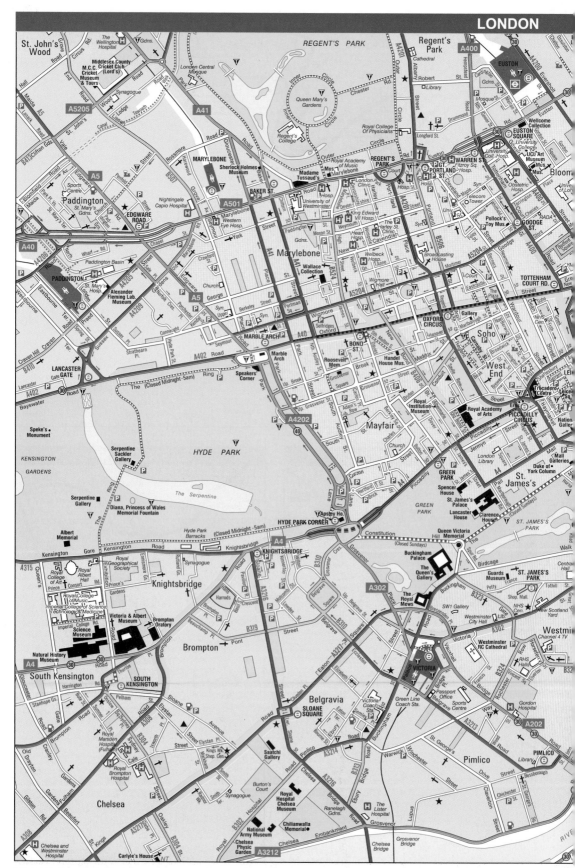

Congestion Charging Zone

■ The daily charge applies Mon.-Fri. 7-00am to 6-00pm excluding English bank and public holidays and designated non-charging days.

■ Payment of the daily charge allows you to drive in, around, leave and re-enter the charging zone as many times as required.

■ You can pay in advance or on the day of travel. If you don't pay by midnight on the charging day after you drove in the zone, you'll get a Penalty Charge Notice.

■ You can pay by telephone (0845 900 1234), via the website (www.tfl.gov.uk), or by SMS.

■ A discount scheme using Congestion Charge Auto Pay is available from Transport for London. (registration required)

■ Exemptions include motorcycles, mopeds and bicycles. Registration for other discount schemes, including Blue Badge holders, residents, greener vehicles and electric vehicles, is also available from Transport for London.

Information correct at time of going to press. For further information www.tfl.gov.uk

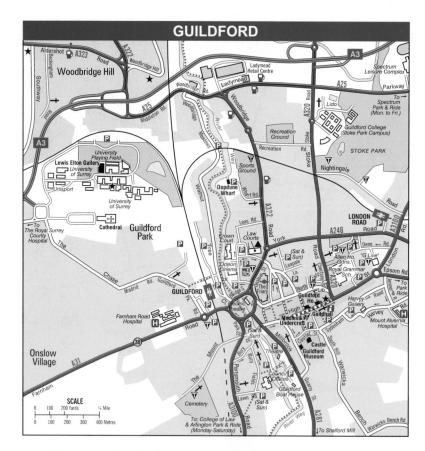

GUILDFORD

MEDWAY TOWNS

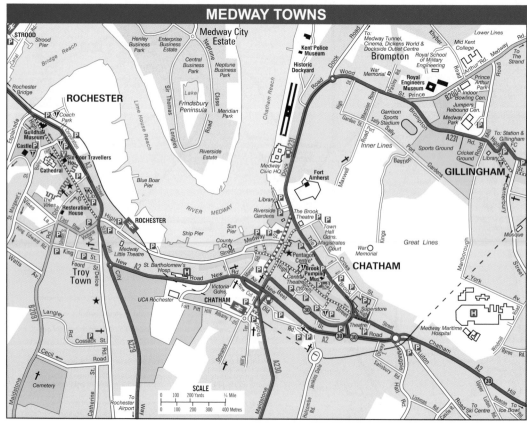

MILTON KEYNES

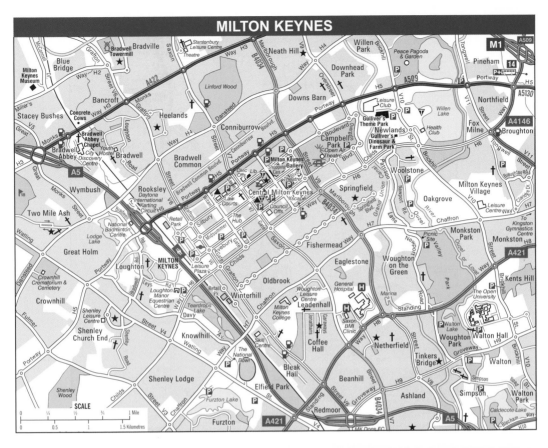

OXFORD

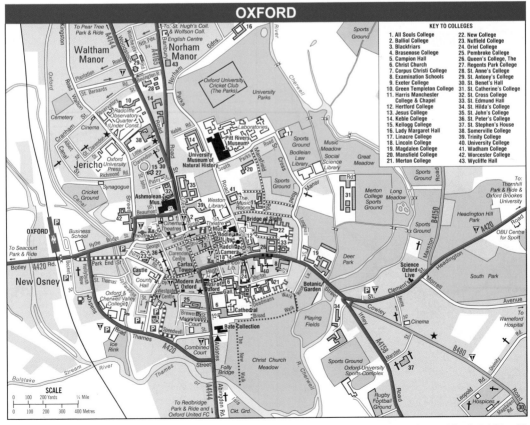

KEY TO COLLEGES

1. All Souls College
2. Balliol College
3. Blackfriars
4. Brasenose College
5. Campion Hall
6. Christ Church
7. Corpus Christi College
8. Examination Schools
9. Exeter College
10. Green Templeton College
11. Harris Manchester College & Chapel
12. Hertford College
13. Jesus College
14. Keble College
15. Kellogg College
16. Lady Margaret Hall
17. Linacre College
18. Lincoln College
19. Magdalen College
20. Mansfield College
21. Merton College
22. New College
23. Nuffield College
24. Oriel College
25. Pembroke College
26. Queen's College, The
27. Regents Park College
28. St. Anne's College
29. St. Antony's College
30. St. Benet's Hall
31. St. Catherine's College
32. St. Cross College
33. St. Edmund Hall
34. St. Hilda's College
35. St. John's College
36. St. Peter's College
37. St. Stephen's House
38. Somerville College
39. Trinity College
40. University College
41. Wadham College
42. Worcester College
43. Wycliffe Hall

PORTSMOUTH

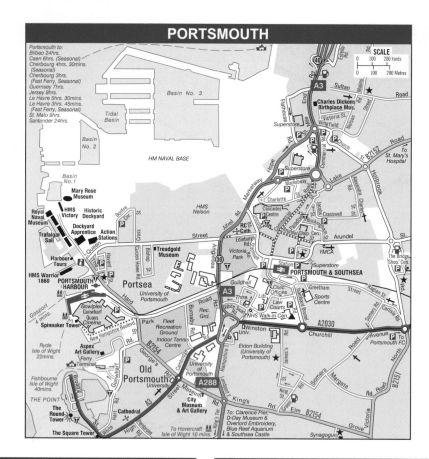

FOLKESTONE

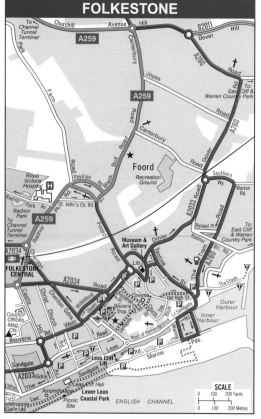

READING

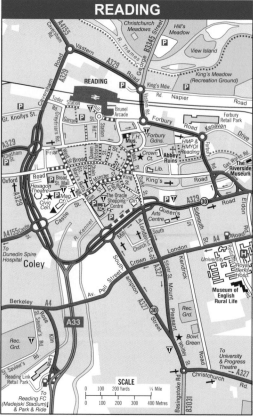

56 *South East England Regional Atlas*

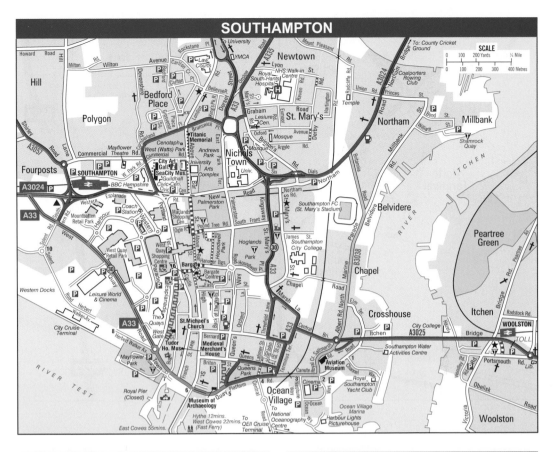

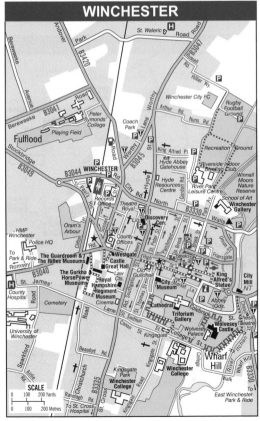

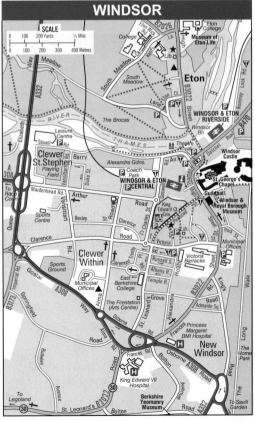

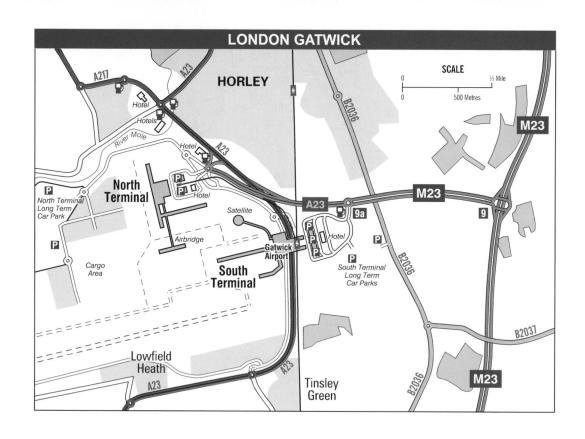

LONDON GATWICK

HORLEY

SCALE

North Terminal

North Terminal Long Term Car Park

River Mole

Cargo Area

Satellite

Airbridge

Gatwick Airport

South Terminal

South Terminal Long Term Car Parks

Lowfield Heath

Tinsley Green

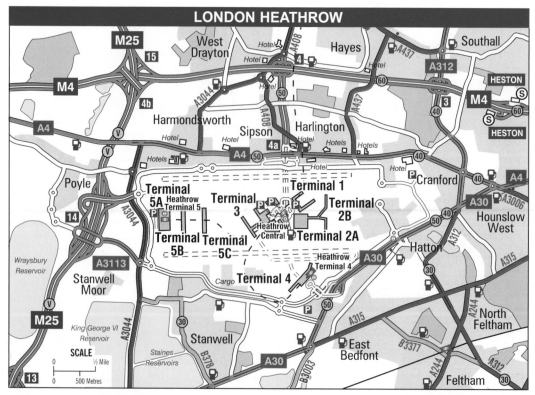

LONDON HEATHROW

West Drayton

Hayes

Southall

HESTON

M4

Harmondsworth

Sipson

Harlington

HESTON

M4

Poyle

Terminal 5A Heathrow Terminal 5

Terminal 3

Terminal 1

Terminal 2B

Cranford

Hounslow West

Terminal 5B

Terminal 5C

Heathrow Central

Terminal 2A

Hatton

Wraysbury Reservoir

Heathrow Terminal 4

Stanwell Moor

King George VI Reservoir

Cargo

Terminal 4

North Feltham

SCALE

Staines Reservoirs

Stanwell

East Bedfont

Feltham

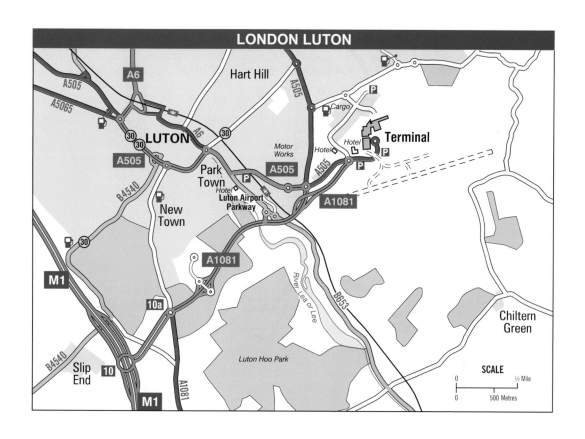

LONDON LUTON

- Hart Hill
- A6
- A505
- A5065
- LUTON
- A505
- A6
- Motor Works
- Cargo
- Hotel
- Hotel
- Terminal
- P
- P
- Park Town
- A505
- A505
- Hotel
- Luton Airport Parkway
- A1081
- New Town
- A1081
- M1
- 10a
- B4540
- B4540
- Slip End
- 10
- M1
- A1081
- River Lea or Lee
- B653
- Luton Hoo Park
- Chiltern Green

SCALE
0 — ½ Mile
0 — 500 Metres

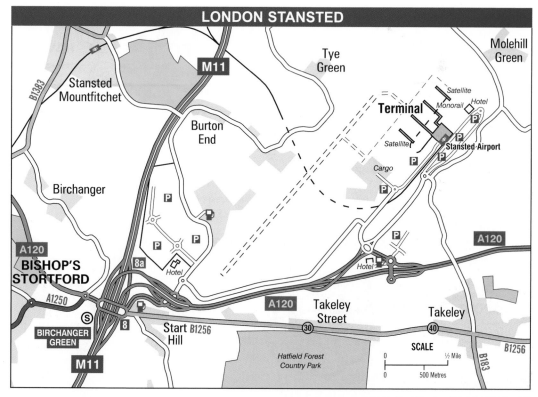

LONDON STANSTED

- B1383
- M11
- Tye Green
- Molehill Green
- Stansted Mountfitchet
- Burton End
- Satellite
- Monorail
- Hotel
- P
- Terminal
- Satellite
- Stansted Airport
- Satellite
- Cargo
- P
- P
- Birchanger
- P
- P
- P
- A120
- A120
- BISHOP'S STORTFORD
- 8a
- Hotel
- Hotel
- A120
- A1250
- S
- 8
- Start Hill
- B1256
- Takeley Street
- 30
- Takeley
- 40
- BIRCHANGER GREEN
- M11
- Hatfield Forest Country Park
- B1256
- B183

SCALE
0 — ½ Mile
0 — 500 Metres

South East England Regional Atlas 59

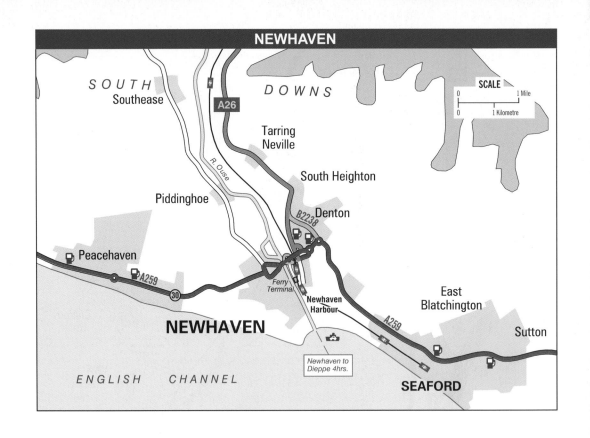

SOUTH DOWNS

Southease

A26

Tarring Neville

R. Ouse

South Heighton

B2238

Denton

Piddinghoe

Peacehaven

A259

30

Ferry Terminal

Newhaven Harbour

NEWHAVEN

East Blatchington

A259

Sutton

Newhaven to Dieppe 4hrs.

ENGLISH CHANNEL

SEAFORD

SCALE
0   1 Mile
0   1 Kilometre

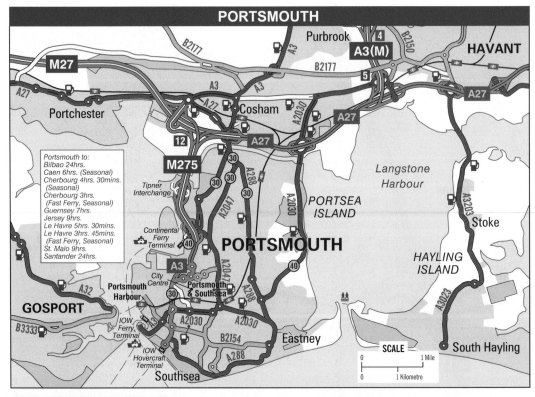

B2177

A3

Purbrook

4

B2150

HAVANT

M27

A3(M)

B2177

5

A27

A27

Cosham

A2030

A27

Portchester

A3

A3

A27

A27

Portsmouth to:
Bilbao 24hrs.
Caen 6hrs. (Seasonal)
Cherbourg 4hrs. 30mins.
(Seasonal)
Cherbourg 3hrs.
(Fast Ferry, Seasonal)
Guernsey 7hrs.
Jersey 9hrs.
Le Havre 5hrs. 30mins.
Le Havre 3hrs. 45mins.
(Fast Ferry, Seasonal)
St. Malo 9hrs.
Santander 24hrs.

12

M275

Tipner Interchange

30

30

30

A288

30

Langstone Harbour

A2030

PORTSEA ISLAND

A32047

HAYLING ISLAND

A3203

Stoke

Continental Ferry Terminal

40

PORTSMOUTH

40

A3

City Centre

Portsmouth & Southsea

30

A2041

A288

GOSPORT

A32

Portsmouth Harbour

B3333

IOW Ferry Terminal

A2030

A2030

B2154

Eastney

A3023

IOW Hovercraft Terminal

A288

Southsea

South Hayling

SCALE
0   1 Mile
0   1 Kilometre

INDEX TO CITIES, TOWNS, VILLAGES, HAMLETS & LOCATIONS

(1) A strict alphabetical order is used e.g. Eastchurch follows East Chiltington but precedes East Clandon.

(2) The map reference given refers to the actual map square in which the town spot or built-up area is located and not to the place name.

(3) Only one reference is given although due to page overlaps the place may appear on more than one page.

(4) Where two places of the same name occur in the same County or Unitary Authority, the nearest large town is also given;
e.g. Ash. *Kent* . . . .3C **31** (nr. Sandwich) indicates that Ash is located in square 3C on page **31** and is situated near Sandwich in the County of Kent.

(5) Major towns and destinations are shown in bold i.e. **Brighton.** *Brig* . . . .2B **46** & **50**. Where they appear on a Town Plan a second page reference is given.

COUNTIES AND UNITARY AUTHORITIES with the abbreviations used in this index

Bedford : *Bed*
Bracknell Forest : *Brac*
Brighton & Hove : *Brig*
Buckinghamshire : *Buck*
Cambridgeshire : *Cambs*
Central Bedfordshire : *C Beds*
Cumbria : *Cumb*
East Sussex : *E Sus*
Essex : *Essx*
Greater London : *G Lon*
Hampshire : *Hants*
Hertfordshire : *Herts*
Isle of Wight : *IOW*
Kent : *Kent*
Luton : *Lutn*
Medway : *Medw*
Milton Keynes : *Mil*
Northamptonshire : *Nptn*
Oxfordshire : *Oxon*
Portsmouth : *Port*
Reading : *Read*
Slough : *Slo*
Southampton : *Sotn*
Southend-on-Sea : *S'end*
Suffolk : *Suff*
Surrey : *Surr*
Thurrock : *Thur*
West Berkshire : *W Ber*
West Sussex : *W Sus*
Windsor & Maidenhead : *Wind*
Wokingham : *Wok*

A

Abberton. *Essx* 3A **12**
Abbess Roding. *Essx* 3D **9**
Abbey Wood. *G Lon* 1C **27**
Abbots Langley. *Herts* 1C **17**
Abbotstone. *Hants* 2B **32**
Abbots Worthy. *Hants* 2A **32**
Abingdon-on-Thames. *Oxon* 2A **14**
Abinger Common. *Surr* 1D **35**
Abinger Hammer. *Surr* 1C **35**
Abridge. *Essx* 2C **19**
Acol. *Kent* 2D **31**
Acrise. *Kent* 1B **40**
Acton. *G Lon* 3D **17**
Adderbury. *Oxon* 1A **4**
Addington. *Buck* 2D **5**
Addington. *G Lon* 2B **26**
Addington. *Kent* 3A **28**
Addiscombe. *G Lon* 2B **26**
Addlestone. *Surr* 2C **25**
Adgestone. *IOW* 3B **42**
Adisham. *Kent* 3C **31**
Adstock. *Buck* 1D **5**
Adversane. *W Sus* 3C **35**
Adwell. *Oxon* 2C **15**
Aingers Green. *Essx* 2B **12**
Akeley. *Buck* 1D **5**
Albourne. *W Sus* 1A **46**
Albury. *Herts* 2C **9**
Albury. *Surr* 1C **35**
Alciston. *E Sus* 2D **47**
Aldbury. *Herts* 3B **6**
Aldenham. *Herts* 2D **17**
Aldermaston. *W Ber* 2B **22**
Aldermaston Stoke. *W Ber* 2C **23**
Aldermaston Wharf. *W Ber* 2C **23**
Aldershot. *Hants* 3A **24**
Alderton. *Suff* 1D **13**
Aldham. *Essx* 2D **11**
Aldingbourne. *W Sus* 2B **44**
Aldington. *Kent* 2A **40**
Aldington Frith. *Kent* 2A **40**
Aldsworth. *W Sus* 2D **43**
Aldwick. *W Sus* 3B **44**
Aldworth. *W Ber* 1B **22**
Aley Green. *C Beds* 3C **7**
Alfold. *Surr* 2C **35**
Alfold Bars. *W Sus* 2C **35**
Alfold Crossways. *Surr* 2C **35**
Alfriston. *E Sus* 2D **47**
Alkerton. *Oxon* 1A **4**
Alkham. *Kent* 1C **41**
Allbrook. *Hants* 3A **32**
Allen's Green. *Herts* 3C **9**
Allhallows. *Medw* 1C **29**
Allhallows-on-Sea. *Medw* 1C **29**
Allington. *Kent* 3B **28**
Almodington. *W Sus* 3A **44**
Alphamstone. *Essx* 1C **11**
Alresford. *Essx* 2A **12**
Althorne. *Essx* 2D **21**
Alton. *Hants* 2D **33**
Alverstoke. *Hants* 3B **42**
Amberley. *W Sus* 1C **45**
Ambrosden. *Oxon* 3C **5**
Amersham. *Buck* 2B **16**
Ampfield. *Hants* 3A **32**
Ampthill. *C Beds* 1C **7**
Amwell. *Herts* 3D **7**
Ancton. *W Sus* 2B **44**
Andover. *Hants* 1A **32**
Andover Down. *Hants* 1A **32**
Andwell. *Hants* 3C **23**
Angmering. *W Sus* 2C **45**
Angmering-on-Sea. *W Sus* 2C **45**
Anmore. *Hants* 1C **43**
Ansteadbrook. *Surr* 2B **34**
Anstey. *Herts* 1C **9**
Ansty. *W Sus* 3A **36**
Anthill Common. *Hants* 1C **43**
Appledore. *Kent* 3D **39**
Appledore Heath. *Kent* 2D **39**
Appleford. *Oxon* 2B **14**
Applemore. *Hants* 2A **42**
Appleton. *Oxon* 1A **14**
Apsley End. *C Beds* 1D **7**
Apuldram. *W Sus* 2A **44**
Arborfield. *Wok* 2D **23**
Arborfield Cross. *Wok* 2D **23**
Arborfield Garrison. *Wok* 2D **23**
Ardeley. *Herts* 2B **8**
Ardingly. *W Sus* 3B **36**
Ardington. *Oxon* 3A **14**
Ardleigh. *Essx* 2A **12**
Ardley. *Oxon* 2B **4**
Arford. *Hants* 2A **34**
Arkesden. *Essx* 1C **9**
Arkley. *G Lon* 2A **18**
Arlesey. *C Beds* 1D **7**
Arlington. *E Sus* 2D **47**
Arreton. *IOW* 3B **42**
Artington. *Surr* 1B **34**
Arundel. *W Sus* 2C **45**
Ascot. *Wind* 2B **24**
Ash. *Kent* 3C **31** (nr. Sandwich)
Ash. *Kent* 2A **28** (nr. Swanley)
Ash. *Surr* 3A **24**
Ashampstead. *W Ber* 1B **22**
Ashdon. *Essx* 1D **9**
Ashe. *Hants* 3B **22**
Asheldham. *Essx* 1D **21**
Ashen. *Essx* 1B **10**
Ashendon. *Buck* 3D **5**
Ashey. *IOW* 3B **42**
Ashfield. *Hants* 1A **42**
Ashfold Crossways. *W Sus* 3A **36**
Ashford. *Kent* 1A **40**
Ashford. *Surr* 1C **25**
Ashford Hill. *Hants* 2B **22**
Ashingdon. *Essx* 2C **21**
Ashington. *W Sus* 1D **45**
Ashlett. *Hants* 2A **42**
Ashley. *Hants* 2A **32**
Ashley. *Kent* 1D **41**
Ashley Green. *Buck* 1B **16**
Ashmansworth. *Hants* 3A **22**
Ashmore Green. *W Ber* 2B **22**
Ashtead. *Surr* 3D **25**
Ashurst. *Kent* 2D **37**
Ashurst. *W Sus* 1D **45**
Ashurst Wood. *W Sus* 2C **37**
Ash Vale. *Surr* 3A **24**
Ashwell. *Herts* 1A **8**
Askett. *Buck* 1A **16**
Aspenden. *Herts* 2B **8**
Aspley Guise. *C Beds* 1B **6**
Aspley Heath. *C Beds* 1B **6**
Assington. *Suff* 1D **11**
Aston. *Herts* 2A **8**
Aston. *Wok* 3D **15**
Aston Abbotts. *Buck* 2A **6**
Aston Clinton. *Buck* 3A **6**
Aston End. *Herts* 2A **8**
Aston Rowant. *Oxon* 2D **15**
Aston Sandford. *Buck* 1D **15**
Aston Tirrold. *Oxon* 3B **14**
Aston Upthorpe. *Oxon* 3B **14**
Astrop. *Nptn* 1B **4**
Astwick. *C Beds* 1A **8**
Atherington. *W Sus* 2C **45**
Audley End. *Essx* 1D **9**
Aveley. *Thur* 3D **19**
Avington. *Hants* 2B **32**
Axford. *Hants* 1C **33**
Aylesbury. *Buck* 3A **6**
Aylesford. *Kent* 3B **28**
Aylesham. *Kent* 3C **31**
Aynho. *Nptn* 1B **4**
Ayot Green. *Herts* 3A **8**
Ayot St Lawrence. *Herts* 3D **7**
Ayot St Peter. *Herts* 3A **8**

B

Babb's Green. *Herts* 3B **8**
Bablock Hythe. *Oxon* 1A **14**
Bacon End. *Essx* 3A **10**
Badgers Mount. *Kent* 2C **27**
Badlesmere. *Kent* 3A **30**
Badshot Lea. *Surr* 1A **34**
Bagham. *Kent* 3A **30**
Bagnor. *W Ber* 2A **22**
Bagshot. *Surr* 2B **24**
Bailey Green. *Hants* 3C **33**
Bainton. *Oxon* 2B **4**
Baker Street. *Thur* 3A **20**
Balcombe. *W Sus* 2B **36**
Balcombe Lane. *W Sus* 2B **36**
Baldock. *Herts* 1A **8**
Baldslow. *E Sus* 1C **49**
Ballards Gore. *Essx* 2D **21**
Ball Hill. *Hants* 2A **22**
Ballingdon. *Suff* 1C **11**
Ballinger Common. *Buck* 1B **16**
Balls Cross. *W Sus* 3B **34**
Ball's Green. *E Sus* 2C **37**
Balscote. *Oxon* 1A **4**
Balstonia. *Thur* 3A **20**
Bamber's Green. *Essx* 2D **9**
Banbury. *Oxon* 1A **4**
Bannister Green. *Essx* 2A **10**
Banstead. *Surr* 3A **26**
Bapchild. *Kent* 2D **29**
Barcombe. *E Sus* 1C **47**
Barcombe Cross. *E Sus* 1C **47**
Bardfield End Green. *Essx* 1A **10**
Bardfield Saling. *Essx* 2A **10**
Barford. *Hants* 2A **34**
Barford St John. *Oxon* 1A **4**
Barford St Michael. *Oxon* 1A **4**
Barfrestone. *Kent* 3C **31**
Barham. *Kent* 3C **31**
Barkham. *Wok* 2D **23**
Barking. *G Lon* 3C **19**
Barkingside. *G Lon* 3C **19**
Barkway. *Herts* 1B **8**
Barlavington. *W Sus* 1B **44**
Barley. *Herts* 1B **8**
Barling. *Essx* 3D **21**
Barming. *Kent* 3B **28**
Barming Heath. *Kent* 3B **28**
Barnard Gate. *Oxon* 3A **4**
Barnes. *G Lon* 1A **26**
Barnes Street. *Kent* 1A **38**
Barnet. *G Lon* 2A **18**
Barnham. *W Sus* 2B **44**
Barns Green. *W Sus* 3D **35**
Barnston. *Essx* 3A **10**
Bartholomew Green. *Essx* 2B **10**
Barton. *IOW* 3B **42**
Barton. *Oxon* 1B **14**
Barton Hartsthorn. *Buck* 1C **5**
Barton-le-Clay. *C Beds* 1C **7**
Barton Stacey. *Hants* 1A **32**
Barwick. *Herts* 3B **8**
Basildon. *Essx* 3B **20**
Basingstoke. *Hants* 3C **23**
Bassett. *Sotn* 1A **42**
Bassingbourn. *Cambs* 1B **8**
Bassus Green. *Herts* 2B **8**
Batchworth. *Herts* 2C **17**
Battersea. *G Lon* 1A **26**
Battle. *E Sus* 1B **48**
Battlesbridge. *Essx* 2B **20**
Battlesden. *C Beds* 2B **6**
Batt's Corner. *Surr* 1A **34**
Baughurst. *Hants* 2B **22**
Bawdsey. *Suff* 1D **13**
Bawdsey Manor. *Suff* 1D **13**
Baybridge. *Hants* 3B **32**
Bayford. *Herts* 1B **18**
Baynard's Green. *Oxon* 2B **4**
Baythorn End. *Essx* 1B **10**
Bayworth. *Oxon* 1B **14**
Beachampton. *Buck* 1D **5**
Beacon End. *Essx* 2D **11**
Beacon Hill. *Surr* 2A **34**
Beacon's Bottom. *Buck* 2D **15**
Beaconsfield. *Buck* 2B **16**
Beacontree. *G Lon* 3C **19**
Beamond End. *Buck* 2B **16**
Bean. *Kent* 1D **27**
Beanshanger. *Nptn* 1D **5**
Beare Green. *Surr* 1D **35**
Bearsted. *Kent* 3B **28**
Beauchamp Roding. *Essx* 3D **9**
Beaulieu. *Hants* 2A **42**
Beaumont. *Essx* 2B **12**
Beauworth. *Hants* 3B **32**
Beazley End. *Essx* 2B **10**
Beckenham. *G Lon* 2B **26**
Beckley. *E Sus* 3C **39**
Beckley. *Oxon* 3B **4**
Beckton. *G Lon* 3C **19**
Becontree. *G Lon* 3C **19**
Beddingham. *E Sus* 2C **47**
Beddington. *G Lon* 2A **26**
Bedham. *W Sus* 3C **35**
Bedhampton. *Hants* 2D **43**
Bedlar's Green. *Essx* 3D **9**
Bedmond. *Herts* 1C **17**
Beech. *Hants* 2C **33**
Beech Hill. *W Ber* 2C **23**
Beedon. *W Ber* 1A **22**
Beenham. *W Ber* 2B **22**
Begbroke. *Oxon* 3A **4**
Beggar Hill. *Essx* 1A **20**
Bekesbourne. *Kent* 3B **30**
Belchamp Otten. *Essx* 1C **11**
Belchamp St Paul. *Essx* 1B **10**
Belchamp Walter. *Essx* 1C **11**
Bellingdon. *Buck* 1B **16**
Bells Yew Green. *E Sus* 2A **38**
Belsize. *Herts* 1C **17**
Belstead. *Suff* 1B **12**
Beltinge. *Kent* 2B **30**
Beltring. *Kent* 1A **38**
Belvedere. *G Lon* 1C **27**
Bembridge. *IOW* 3C **43**
Bendish. *Herts* 2D **7**
Benenden. *Kent* 2C **39**
Benington. *Herts* 2A **8**
Benover. *Kent* 1B **38**
Benson. *Oxon* 2C **15**
Bentley. *Hants* 1D **33**
Bentley. *Suff* 1B **12**
Bentley Heath. *Herts* 2A **18**
Bentworth. *Hants* 1C **33**
Bepton. *W Sus* 1A **44**
Berden. *Essx* 2C **9**
Berinsfield. *Oxon* 2B **14**
Berkhamsted. *Herts* 1B **16**
Bermondsey. *G Lon* 1B **26**
Berrick Salome. *Oxon* 2C **15**
Berry's Green. *G Lon* 3C **27**
Berwick. *E Sus* 2D **47**
Bessels Leigh. *Oxon* 1A **14**
Best Beech Hill. *E Sus* 2A **38**
Betchworth. *Surr* 3A **26**
Bethersden. *Kent* 1D **39**
Bethnal Green. *G Lon* 3B **18**
Betsham. *Kent* 1A **28**
Betteshanger. *Kent* 3D **31**
Bevendean. *Brig* 2B **46**
Bexhill. *E Sus* 2B **48**
Bexley. *G Lon* 1C **27**
Bexleyheath. *G Lon* 1C **27**
Bexleyhill. *W Sus* 3B **34**
Bicester. *Oxon* 2B **4**
Bicknacre. *Essx* 1B **20**
Bicknor. *Kent* 3C **29**
Bidborough. *Kent* 1D **37**
Biddenden. *Kent* 2C **39**
Biddenden Green. *Kent* 1C **39**
Biddlesden. *Buck* 1C **5**
Bierton. *Buck* 3A **6**
Biggin Hill. *G Lon* 3C **27**

Biggleswade—Charleshill

Biggleswade. *C Beds* 1A **8**
Bighton. *Hants* 2C **33**
Bignor. *W Sus* 1B **44**
Billericay. *Essx* 2A **20**
Billingshurst. *W Sus* 3C **35**
Billington. *C Beds* 2B **6**
Bilsham. *W Sus* 2B **44**
Bilsington. *Kent* 2A **40**
Bilting. *Kent* 1A **40**
Bines Green. *W Sus* 1D **45**
Binfield. *Brac* 1A **24**
Binfield Heath. *Oxon* 1D **23**
Binley. *Hants* 3A **22**
Binstead. *IOW* 3B **42**
Binstead. *W Sus* 2B **44**
Binsted. *Hants* 1D **33**
Birch. *Essx* 3D **11**
Birchanger. *Essx* 2D **9**
Birch Green. *Essx* 3D **11**
Birchington. *Kent* 2C **31**
Birchmoor Green. *C Beds* 1B **6**
Birdbrook. *Essx* 1B **10**
Birdham. *W Sus* 2A **44**
Birds Green. *Essx* 1D **19**
Birling. *Kent* 2A **28**
Birling Gap. *E Sus* 3D **47**
Bisham. *Wind* 3A **16**
Bishopsbourne. *Kent* 3B **30**
Bishop's Green. *Essx* 3A **10**
Bishop's Green. *Hants* 2B **22**
Bishop's Stortford. *Herts* 2C **9**
Bishops Sutton. *Hants* 2C **33**
Bishopstoke. *Hants* 1A **42**
Bishopstone. *Buck* 3A **6**
Bishopstone. *E Sus* 2C **47**
Bishop's Waltham. *Hants* 1B **42**
Bisley. *Surr* 3B **24**
Bitterne. *Sotn* 1A **42**
Bix. *Oxon* 3D **15**
Blackboys. *E Sus* 3D **37**
Blackbrook. *Surr* 1D **35**
Blackditch. *Oxon* 1A **14**
Blackfen. *G Lon* 1C **27**
Blackfield. *Hants* 2A **42**
Blackham. *E Sus* 2C **37**
Blackheath. *Essx* 2A **12**
Blackheath. *G Lon* 1B **26**
Blackheath. *Surr* 1C **35**
Blackmoor. *Hants* 2D **33**
Blackmore. *Essx* 1A **20**
Blackmore End. *Essx* 1B **10**
Blackmore End. *Herts* 3D **7**
Blacknest. *Hants* 1D **33**
Black Notley. *Essx* 2B **10**
Blackstone. *W Sus* 1A **46**
Blackthorn. *Oxon* 3C **5**
Blackwall Tunnel. *G Lon* 3B **18**
Blackwater. *Hants* 3A **24**
Blackwater. *IOW* 3B **42**
Bladon. *Oxon* 3A **4**
Blake End. *Essx* 2B **10**
Blean. *Kent* 2B **30**
Bledlow. *Buck* 1D **15**
Bledlow Ridge. *Buck* 2D **15**
Blendworth. *Hants* 1D **43**
Blenheim. *Oxon* 1B **14**
Bletchingdon. *Oxon* 3B **4**
Bletchingley. *Surr* 3B **26**
Bletchley. *Mil* 1A **6**
Blewbury. *Oxon* 3B **14**
Blindley Heath. *Surr* 1B **36**
Bloxham. *Oxon* 1A **4**
Blue Bell Hill. *Kent* 2B **28**
Blue Row. *Essx* 3A **12**
Bluetown. *Kent* 3D **29**
Boarhunt. *Hants* 2C **43**
Boarshead. *E Sus* 2D **37**
Boars Hill. *Oxon* 1A **14**
Boarstall. *Buck* 3C **5**
Bobbing. *Kent* 2C **29**
Bobbingworth. *Essx* 1D **19**
Bocking. *Essx* 2B **10**
Bocking Churchstreet. *Essx* 2B **10**
Bodiam. *E Sus* 3B **38**
Bodicote. *Oxon* 1A **4**
Bodle Street Green. *E Sus* 1A **48**
Bodsham. *Kent* 1B **40**
Bognor Regis. *W Sus* 3B **44**
Bolney. *W Sus* 3A **36**
Bonnington. *Kent* 2A **40**
Booker. *Buck* 2A **16**
Boorley Green. *Hants* 1B **42**
Borden. *Kent* 2C **29**
Borden. *W Sus* 3A **34**
Bordon. *Hants* 2A **34**
Boreham. *Essx* 1B **20**
Boreham Street. *E Sus* 1A **48**
Borehamwood. *Herts* 2D **17**
Borley. *Essx* 1C **11**
Borley Green. *Essx* 1C **11**
Borough Green. *Kent* 3A **28**
Borstal. *Medw* 2B **28**
Bosham. *W Sus* 2A **44**
Bossingham. *Kent* 1B **40**
Botany Bay. *G Lon* 2A **18**
Bothampstead. *W Ber* 1B **22**
Botley. *Buck* 1B **16**
Botley. *Hants* 1B **42**
Botley. *Oxon* 1A **14**
Botolph Claydon. *Buck* 2D **5**
Botolphs. *W Sus* 2D **45**
Bough Beech. *Kent* 1C **37**
Boughton Aluph. *Kent* 1A **40**
Boughton Green. *Kent* 3B **28**
Boughton Lees. *Kent* 1A **40**
Boughton Malherbe. *Kent* 1C **39**
Boughton Monchelsea. *Kent* 3B **28**
Boughton under Blean. *Kent* 3A **30**
Bouldnor. *IOW* 3A **42**
Bourne End. *Buck* 3A **16**
Bourne End. *Herts* 1C **17**
Bournes Green. *S'end* 3D **21**
Bourne, The. *Surr* 1A **34**
Boveney. *Buck* 1B **24**
Bovingdon. *Herts* 1C **17**
Bovingdon Green. *Buck* 3A **16**
Bovinger. *Essx* 1D **19**
Bow Brickhill. *Mil* 1B **6**
Bowcombe. *IOW* 3A **42**
Bowers Gifford. *Essx* 3B **20**
Bowlhead Green. *Surr* 2B **34**
Boxford. *Suff* 1D **11**
Boxford. *W Ber* 1A **22**
Boxgrove. *W Sus* 2B **44**
Boxley. *Kent* 3B **28**
Boxmoor. *Herts* 1C **17**
Boxted. *Essx* 1D **11**
Boxted Cross. *Essx* 1A **12**
Boyden Gate. *Kent* 2C **31**
Boyton Cross. *Essx* 1A **20**
Boyton End. *Essx* 1A **10**
Brabourne. *Kent* 1B **40**
Brabourne Lees. *Kent* 1A **40**
Bracklesham. *W Sus* 3A **44**
Brackley. *Nptn* 1B **4**
Brackley Hatch. *Nptn* 1C **5**
Bracknell. *Brac* 2A **24**
Bradenham. *Buck* 2A **16**
Bradfield. *Essx* 1B **12**
Bradfield. *W Ber* 1C **23**
Bradfield Heath. *Essx* 2B **12**
Brading. *IOW* 3C **43**
Bradley. *Hants* 1C **33**
Bradwell. *Essx* 2C **11**
Bradwell. *Mil* 1A **6**
Bradwell-on-Sea. *Essx* 3A **12**
Bradwell Waterside. *Essx* 1D **21**
Bragbury End. *Herts* 2A **8**
Braintree. *Essx* 2B **10**
Braishfield. *Hants* 3A **32**
Bramber. *W Sus* 1D **45**
Brambledown. *Kent* 1D **29**
Brambridge. *Hants* 3A **32**
Bramdean. *Hants* 3C **33**
Bramfield. *Herts* 3A **8**
Bramley. *Hants* 3C **23**
Bramley. *Surr* 1C **35**
Bramley Green. *Hants* 3C **23**
Bramling. *Kent* 3C **31**
Bramshill. *Hants* 2D **23**
Bramshott. *Hants* 2A **34**
Bran End. *Essx* 2A **10**
Bransbury. *Hants* 1A **32**
Brantham. *Suff* 1B **12**
Brasted. *Kent* 3C **27**
Brasted Chart. *Kent* 3C **27**
Braughing. *Herts* 2B **8**
Bray. *Wind* 1B **24**
Bray Wick. *Wind* 1A **24**
Breach. *W Sus* 2D **43**
Breachwood Green. *Herts* 2D **7**
Brede. *E Sus* 1C **49**
Bredgar. *Kent* 2C **29**
Bredhurst. *Kent* 2B **28**
Brenchley. *Kent* 1A **38**
Brent Cross. *G Lon* 3A **18**
Brentford. *G Lon* 1D **25**
Brent Pelham. *Herts* 1C **9**
Brentwood. *Essx* 2A **20**
Brenzett. *Kent* 3A **40**
Brewer Street. *Surr* 3B **26**
Bricket Wood. *Herts* 1D **17**
Bridge. *Kent* 3B **30**
Bridge Green. *Essx* 1C **9**
Bridgemary. *Hants* 2B **42**
Brighthampton. *Oxon* 1A **14**
Brightling. *E Sus* 3A **38**
Brightlingsea. *Essx* 3A **12**
Brighton. *Brig* 2B **46** & **50**
Brighton Hill. *Hants* 1C **33**
Brightwalton. *W Ber* 1A **22**
Brightwalton Green. *W Ber* 1A **22**
Brightwell. *Suff* 1C **13**
Brightwell Baldwin. *Oxon* 2C **15**
Brightwell-cum-Sotwell. *Oxon* 2B **14**
Brill. *Buck* 3C **5**
Brimpton. *W Ber* 2B **22**
Brissenden Green. *Kent* 2D **39**
Britwell Salome. *Oxon* 2C **15**
Brixton. *G Lon* 1B **26**
Broadbridge. *W Sus* 2A **44**
Broadbridge Heath. *W Sus* 2D **35**
Broadfield. *W Sus* 2A **36**
Broadford Bridge. *W Sus* 3C **35**
Broad Green. *C Beds* 1B **6**
Broad Laying. *Hants* 2A **22**
Broadley Common. *Essx* 1C **19**
Broadmere. *Hants* 1C **33**
Broad Oak. *E Sus* 1C **49** (nr. Hastings)
Broad Oak. *E Sus* 3A **38** (nr. Heathfield)
Broadoak. *Hants* 1A **42**
Broad Oak. *Kent* 2B **30**
Broad's Green. *Essx* 3A **10**
Broadstairs. *Kent* 2D **31**
Broad Street. *E Sus* 1C **49**
Broad Street. *Kent* 1B **40** (nr. Ashford)
Broad Street. *Kent* 3C **29** (nr. Maidstone)
Broad Street Green. *Essx* 1C **21**
Brockbridge. *Hants* 1C **43**
Brockham. *Surr* 1D **35**
Brockhurst. *Hants* 2B **42**
Brogborough. *C Beds* 1B **6**
Bromley. *G Lon* 2C **27**
Bromley. *Herts* 2C **9**
Bromley Green. *Kent* 2D **39**
Brompton. *Medw* 2B **28**
Brook. *Kent* 1A **40**
Brook. *Surr* 1C **35** (nr. Guildford)
Brook. *Surr* 2B **34** (nr. Haslemere)
Brookland. *Kent* 3D **39**
Brookmans Park. *Herts* 1A **18**
Brooks Green. *W Sus* 3D **35**
Brook Street. *Essx* 2D **19**
Brook Street. *Kent* 2D **39**
Brook Street. *W Sus* 3B **36**
Brookwood. *Surr* 3B **24**
Broom. *C Beds* 1D **7**
Broomer's Corner. *W Sus* 3D **35**
Broomfield. *Essx* 3B **10**
Broomfield. *Kent* 2B **30** (nr. Herne Bay)
Broomfield. *Kent* 3C **29** (nr. Maidstone)
Broomhall. *Wind* 2B **24**
Broughton. *Mil* 1A **6**
Broughton. *Oxon* 1A **4**
Brownbread Street. *E Sus* 1A **48**
Brown Candover. *Hants* 2B **32**
Broxbourne. *Herts* 1B **18**
Broxted. *Essx* 2D **9**
Broyle Side. *E Sus* 1C **47**
Bryant's Bottom. *Buck* 2A **16**
Buckhurst Hill. *Essx* 2C **19**
Buckingham. *Buck* 1C **5**
Buckland. *Buck* 3A **6**
Buckland. *Herts* 1B **8**
Buckland. *Kent* 1D **41**
Buckland. *Oxon* 2A **14**
Buckland. *Surr* 3A **26**
Buckland Common. *Buck* 1B **16**
Bucklebury. *W Ber* 1B **22**
Buckler's Hard. *Hants* 3A **42**
Bucklesham. *Suff* 1C **13**
Bucknell. *Oxon* 2B **4**
Bucks Green. *W Sus* 2C **35**
Bucks Hill. *Herts* 1C **17**
Bucks Horn Oak. *Hants* 1A **34**
Buffler's Holt. *Buck* 1C **5**
Bulbourne. *Herts* 3B **6**
Bull's Green. *Herts* 3A **8**
Bulmer. *Essx* 1C **11**
Bulmer Tye. *Essx* 1C **11**
Bulphan. *Thur* 3A **20**
Bulverhythe. *E Sus* 2B **48**
Bumble's Green. *Essx* 1C **19**
Buntingford. *Herts* 2B **8**
Buntings Green. *Essx* 1C **11**
Burchett's Green. *Wind* 3A **16**
Burcot. *Oxon* 2B **14**
Burcott. *Buck* 2A **6**
Burdrop. *Oxon* 1A **4**
Bures. *Suff* 1D **11**
Burgess Hill. *W Sus* 1B **46**
Burghclere. *Hants* 2A **22**
Burghfield. *W Ber* 2C **23**
Burghfield Common. *W Ber* 2C **23**
Burghfield Hill. *W Ber* 2C **23**
Burgh Heath. *Surr* 3A **26**
Burham. *Kent* 2B **28**
Buriton. *Hants* 3D **33**
Burleigh. *Brac* 1B **24**
Burmarsh. *Kent* 2B **40**
Burnham. *Buck* 3B **16**
Burnham Green. *Herts* 3A **8**
Burnham-on-Crouch. *Essx* 2D **21**
Burntcommon. *Surr* 3C **25**
Burnt Heath. *Essx* 2A **12**
Burnt Hill. *W Ber* 1B **22**
Burnt Oak. *G Lon* 2A **18**
Burpham. *Surr* 3C **25**
Burpham. *W Sus* 2C **45**
Burridge. *Hants* 1B **42**
Burrowhill. *Surr* 2B **24**
Bursledon. *Hants* 2A **42**
Burstow. *Surr* 1B **36**
Burton End. *Essx* 2D **9**
Burton's Green. *Essx* 2C **11**
Burwash. *E Sus* 3A **38**
Burwash Common. *E Sus* 3A **38**
Burwash Weald. *E Sus* 3A **38**
Bury. *W Sus* 1C **45**
Bury Green. *Herts* 2C **9**
Busbridge. *Surr* 1B **34**
Bushey. *Herts* 2D **17**
Bushey Heath. *Herts* 2D **17**
Bustard Green. *Essx* 2A **10**
Butcher's Cross. *E Sus* 3D **37**
Butlocks Heath. *Hants* 2A **42**
Buttsash. *Hants* 2A **42**
Butt's Green. *Essx* 1B **20**
Buxted. *E Sus* 3C **37**
Bybrook. *Kent* 1A **40**
Byfleet. *Surr* 2C **25**
Bygrave. *Herts* 1A **8**
Byworth. *W Sus* 3B **34**

C

Caddington. *C Beds* 3C **7**
Cade Street. *E Sus* 3A **38**
Cadmore End. *Buck* 2D **15**
Cadwell. *Herts* 1D **7**
Calais Street. *Suff* 1D **11**
Calbourne. *IOW* 3A **42**
Calcot Row. *W Ber* 1C **23**
Calcott. *Kent* 2B **30**
Caldecote. *Herts* 1A **8**
Caldecott. *Oxon* 2A **14**
Calshot. *Hants* 2A **42**
Calvert. *Buck* 2C **5**
Calverton. *Mil* 1D **5**
Camber. *E Sus* 1D **49**
Camberley. *Surr* 2A **24**
Camberwell. *G Lon* 1B **26**
Camden Town. *G Lon* 3A **18**
Camelsdale. *Surr* 2B **34**
Camps End. *Cambs* 1A **10**
Campton. *C Beds* 1D **7**
Canadia. *E Sus* 1B **48**
Cane End. *Oxon* 1C **23**
Canewdon. *Essx* 2C **21**
Canterbury. *Kent* 3B **30** & **51**
Canvey Island. *Essx* 3B **20**
Capel. *Kent* 1A **38**
Capel. *Surr* 1D **35**
Capel-le-Ferne. *Kent* 2C **41**
Capel St Mary. *Suff* 1A **12**
Carisbrooke. *IOW* 3A **42**
Carshalton. *G Lon* 2A **26**
Cartbridge. *Surr* 3C **25**
Cassington. *Oxon* 3A **4**
Castle Camps. *Cambs* 1A **10**
Castle Green. *Surr* 2B **24**
Castle Hedingham. *Essx* 1B **10**
Castle Hill. *Kent* 1A **38**
Caterham. *Surr* 3B **26**
Catford. *G Lon* 1B **26**
Catherington. *Hants* 1C **43**
Catisfield. *Hants* 2B **42**
Catmore. *W Ber* 3A **14**
Catsfield. *E Sus* 1B **48**
Cattawade. *Suff* 1B **12**
Catteshall. *Surr* 1B **34**
Caulcott. *Oxon* 2B **4**
Caversfield. *Oxon* 2B **4**
Caversham. *Read* 1D **23**
Caversham Heights. *Read* 1C **23**
Chackmore. *Buck* 1C **5**
Chacombe. *Nptn* 1A **4**
Chaddleworth. *W Ber* 1A **22**
Chadwell Heath. *G Lon* 3C **19**
Chadwell St Mary. *Thur* 1A **28**
Chafford Hundred. *Thur* 1A **28**
Chailey. *E Sus* 1B **46**
Chainhurst. *Kent* 1B **38**
Chaldon. *Surr* 3B **26**
Chalfont Common. *Buck* 2C **17**
Chalfont St Giles. *Buck* 2B **16**
Chalfont St Peter. *Buck* 3C **17**
Chalgrove. *Oxon* 2C **15**
Chalk. *Kent* 1A **28**
Chalk End. *Essx* 3A **10**
Challock. *Kent* 3A **30**
Chalton. *C Beds* 2C **7**
Chalton. *Hants* 1D **43**
Chalvington. *E Sus* 2D **47**
Chandler's Cross. *Herts* 2C **17**
Chandler's Ford. *Hants* 3A **32**
Channel Tunnel. *Kent* 2B **40**
Chantry. *Suff* 1B **12**
Chapel End. *C Beds* 1C **7**
Chapel Row. *W Ber* 2B **22**
Chapmore End. *Herts* 3B **8**
Chappel. *Essx* 2C **11**
Charing. *Kent* 1D **39**
Charing Heath. *Kent* 1D **39**
Charing Hill. *Kent* 3D **29**
Charlbury. *Oxon* 3A **4**
Charleshill. *Surr* 1A **34**

Charlton. *G Lon* 1C 27
Charlton. *Hants* 1A 32
Charlton. *Herts* 2D 7
Charlton. *Nptn* 1B 4
Charlton. *Oxon* 3A 14
Charlton. *W Sus* 1A 44
Charlton-on-Otmoor. *Oxon* 3B 4
Charlwood. *Hants* 2C 33
Charlwood. *Surr* 1A 36
Charndon. *Buck* 2C 5
Charney Bassett. *Oxon* 2A 14
Chart Corner. *Kent* 3B 28
Charter Alley. *Hants* 3B 22
Chartham. *Kent* 3B 30
Chartham Hatch. *Kent* 3B 30
Chartridge. *Buck* 1B 16
Chart Sutton. *Kent* 3B 28
Chart, The. *Kent* 3C 27
Charvil. *Wok* 1D 23
Chatham. *Medw* ......2B 28 & **Medway 54**
Chatham Green. *Essx* 3B 10
Chattenden. *Medw* 1B 28
Chattisham. *Suff* 1A 12
Chaulden. *Herts* 1C 17
Chaul End. *C Beds* 2C 7
Chawley. *Oxon* 1A 14
Chawton. *Hants* 2D 33
Cheam. *Surr* 2A 26
Cheapside. *Wind* 2B 24
Chearsley. *Buck* 3D 5
Checkendon. *Oxon* 3C 15
Cheddington. *Buck* 3B 6
Cheeseman's Green. *Kent* 2A 40
Chelmondiston. *Suff* 1C 13
Chelmsford. *Essx* 1B 20
Chelsea. *G Lon* 1A 26
Chelsfield. *G Lon* 2C 27
Chelsham. *Surr* 3B 26
Chelwood Common. *E Sus* 3C 37
Chelwood Gate. *E Sus* 3C 37
Chenies. *Buck* 2C 17
Cheriton. *Hants* 3B 32
Cheriton. *Kent* 2C 41
Cherry Green. *Herts* 2B 8
Chertsey. *Surr* 2C 25
Chesham. *Buck* 1B 16
Chesham Bois. *Buck* 2B 16
Cheshunt. *Herts* 1B 18
Chessington. *G Lon* 2D 25
Chesterton. *Oxon* 2B 4
Chestfield. *Kent* 2B 30
Chetwode. *Buck* 2C 5
Chevening. *Kent* 3C 27
Chichester. *W Sus* 2A 44
Chicksands. *C Beds* 1D 7
Chidden. *Hants* 1C 43
Chiddingfold. *Surr* 2B 34
Chiddingly. *E Sus* 1D 47
Chiddingstone. *Kent* 1D 37
Chiddingstone Causeway. *Kent* 1D 37
Chiddingstone Hoath. *Kent* 1C 37
Chidham. *W Sus* 2D 43
Chieveley. *W Ber* 1A 22
Chignall St James. *Essx* 1A 20
Chignall Smealy. *Essx* 3A 10
Chigwell. *Essx* 2C 19
Chigwell Row. *Essx* 2C 19
Chilbolton. *Hants* 1A 32
Chilcomb. *Hants* 3B 32
Childrey. *Oxon* 3A 14
Childwick Green. *Herts* 3D 7
Chilgrove. *W Sus* 1A 44
Chilham. *Kent* 3A 30
Chilland. *Hants* 2B 32
Chillenden. *Kent* 3C 31
Chilmington Green. *Kent* 1D 39
Chiltern Green. *C Beds* 3D 7
Chilton. *Buck* 3C 5
Chilton. *Oxon* 3A 14
Chilton Candover. *Hants* 1B 32
Chilworth. *Hants* 1A 42
Chilworth. *Surr* 1C 35
Chimney. *Oxon* 1A 14
Chineham. *Hants* 3C 23
Chingford. *G Lon* 2B 18
Chinnor. *Oxon* 1D 15
Chipperfield. *Herts* 1C 17
Chipping. *Herts* 1B 8
Chipping Hill. *Essx* 3C 11
Chipping Ongar. *Essx* 1D 19
Chipstead. *Kent* 3D 27
Chipstead. *Surr* 3A 26
Chisbridge Cross. *Buck* 3A 16
Chiselhampton. *Oxon* 2B 14
Chislehurst. *G Lon* 2C 27
Chislet. *Kent* 2C 31
Chiswell Green. *Herts* 1D 17
Chiswick. *G Lon* 1A 26
Chitcombe. *E Sus* 3C 39
Chithurst. *W Sus* 3A 34
Chobham. *Surr* 2B 24
Cholesbury. *Buck* 1B 16
Cholsey. *Oxon* 3B 14
Chorleywood. *Herts* 2C 17
Chrishall. *Essx* 1C 9
Christmas Common. *Oxon* 2D 15
Chuck Hatch. *E Sus* 2C 37

Church Crookham. *Hants* 3A 24
Church End. *C Beds* 2B 6
(nr. Dunstable)
Church End. *C Beds* 1D 7
(nr. Stotfold)
Church End. *Essx* 2B 10
(nr. Braintree)
Churchend. *Essx* 2A 10
(nr. Great Dunmow)
Church End. *Essx* 1D 9
(nr. Saffron Walden)
Churchend. *Essx* 2D 21
(nr. Southend-on-Sea)
Church End. *Hants* 3C 23
Church Enstone. *Oxon* 2A 4
Church Hanborough. *Oxon* 3A 4
Church Hougham. *Kent* 1C 41
Church Langley. *Essx* 1C 19
Church Norton. *W Sus* 3A 44
Church Street. *Kent* 1B 28
Churt. *Surr* 2A 34
Cippenham. *Slo* 3B 16
City (London) Airport.
G Lon 3C 19
City of London. *G Lon* 3B 18
City, The. *Buck* 2D 15
Clacton-on-Sea. *Essx* 3B 12
Clanfield. *Hants* 1C 43
Clapgate. *Herts* 2C 9
Clapham. *G Lon* 1A 26
Clapham. *W Sus* 2C 45
Clap Hill. *Kent* 2A 40
Clark's Green. *Surr* 2D 35
Clatterford. *IOW* 3A 42
Clavering. *Essx* 1C 9
Clay End. *Herts* 2B 8
Claygate. *Kent* 1B 38
Claygate. *Surr* 2D 25
Claygate Cross. *Kent* 3A 28
Clayhall. *Hants* 3C 43
Clayhill. *E Sus* 3C 39
Clayton. *W Sus* 1B 46
Cleeve. *Oxon* 3C 15
Cleveley. *Oxon* 2A 4
Cliddesden. *Hants* 1C 33
Cliffe. *Medw* 1C 49
Cliff End. *E Sus* 1C 49
Cliffe Woods. *Medw* 1C 28
Cliffsend. *Kent* 2D 31
Clifton. *C Beds* 1D 7
Clifton. *Oxon* 1A 4
Clifton Hampden. *Oxon* 2B 14
Cliftonville. *Kent* 1D 31
Clophill. *C Beds* 1C 7
Clothall. *Herts* 1A 8
Coalhill. *Essx* 2B 20
Coates. *W Sus* 1B 44
Cobham. *Kent* 2A 28
Cobham. *Surr* 2D 25
Cock Clarks. *Essx* 1C 21
Cock Green. *Essx* 3A 10
Cocking. *W Sus* 1A 44
Cocking Causeway. *W Sus* 1A 44
Cockpole Green. *Wind* 3A 16
Codicote. *Herts* 3A 8
Codmore Hill. *W Sus* 3C 35
Cogges. *Oxon* 1A 14
Coggeshall. *Essx* 2C 11
Coggeshall Hamlet. *Essx* 2C 11
Coggins Mill. *E Sus* 3D 37
Colchester. *Essx* 2A 12
Cold Ash. *W Ber* 2B 22
Coldean. *Brig* 2B 46
Colden Common. *Hants* 3A 32
Coldharbour. *Kent* 3D 27
Coldharbour. *Surr* 1D 35
Cold Norton. *Essx* 1C 21
Coldred. *Kent* 1C 41
Coldwaltham. *W Sus* 1C 45
Cole Green. *Herts* 3A 8
Cole Henley. *Hants* 3A 22
Coleman Green. *Herts* 3D 7
Coleman's Hatch. *E Sus* 2C 37
Colemore. *Hants* 2D 33
Coleshill. *Buck* 2B 16
Colgate. *W Sus* 2A 36
Collier Row. *G Lon* 2C 19
Colliers End. *Herts* 2B 8
Collier Street. *Kent* 1B 38
Colnbrook. *Slo* 1C 25
Colne Engaine. *Essx* 1C 11
Colney Heath. *Herts* 1A 18
Colney Street. *Herts* 1D 17
Colt's Hill. *Kent* 1A 38
Colworth. *W Sus* 2B 44
Combe. *Hants* 3A 4
Combe. *W Ber* 2A 22
Compton. *Hants* 3A 32
Compton. *Surr* 1B 34
Compton. *W Ber* 3B 14
Compton. *W Sus* 1D 43
Coneyhurst Common.
W Sus 3D 35
Conford. *Hants* 2A 34

Conyer. *Kent* 2D 29
Cooden. *E Sus* 2B 48
Cookham. *Wind* 3A 16
Cookham Dean. *Wind* 3A 16
Cookham Rise. *Wind* 3A 16
Cookley Green. *Oxon* 2C 15
Cooksbridge. *E Sus* 1C 47
Cooksmill Green. *Essx* 1A 20
Coolham. *W Sus* 3D 35
Cooling. *Medw* 1B 28
Cooling Street. *Medw* 1B 28
Coombe. *Hants* 3C 33
Coombes. *W Sus* 2D 45
Coopersale Common. *Essx* 1C 19
Coopersale Street. *Essx* 1C 19
Cooper's Corner. *Kent* 1C 37
Cooper Street. *Kent* 3D 31
Cootham. *W Sus* 1C 45
Copdock. *Suff* 1B 12
Copford. *Essx* 2D 11
Copford Green. *Essx* 2D 11
Copsale. *W Sus* 3D 35
Copthall Green. *Essx* 1C 19
Copthorne. *W Sus* 2B 36
Corhampton. *Hants* 3C 33
Cornish Hall End. *Essx* 1A 10
Corringham. *Thur* 3B 20
Coryton. *Thur* 3B 20
Coscote. *Oxon* 3B 14
Cosham. *Port* 2A 44
Cosgrove. *Nptn* 1D 5
Cote. *Oxon* 1A 14
Cottiill. *Oxon* 2A 14
Cottered. *Herts* 2B 8
Cottisford. *Oxon* 1B 4
Coulsdon. *Surr* 3A 26
Coultershaw Bridge. *W Sus* 1B 44
Countess Cross. *Essx* 1C 11
Court-at-Street. *Kent* 2A 40
Courtsend. *Essx* 2D 21
Cousley Wood. *E Sus* 2A 38
Cove. *Hants* 3A 24
Cowbeech. *E Sus* 1A 48
Cowden. *Kent* 1C 37
Cowes. *IOW* 3A 42
Cowfold. *W Sus* 3A 36
Cowley. *G Lon* 3C 17
Cowley. *Oxon* 1B 14
Cowplain. *Hants* 1C 43
Cox Green. *Surr* 2C 35
Coxheath. *Kent* 3B 28
Crabtree. *W Sus* 3A 36
Crafton. *Buck* 3A 6
Cranbourne. *Brac* 1B 24
Cranbrook. *Kent* 2B 38
Cranbrook Common. *Kent* 2B 38
Cranfield. *C Beds* 1B 6
Cranford. *G Lon* 1C 25
Cranham. *G Lon* 3D 19
Cranleigh. *Surr* 2C 35
Cranmore. *IOW* 3A 42
Crawley. *Hants* 2A 32
Crawley. *W Sus* 2A 36
Crawley Down. *W Sus* 2B 36
Crayford. *G Lon* 1D 27
Crays Hill. *Essx* 2B 20
Cray's Pond. *Oxon* 3C 15
Crazies Hill. *Wok* 3D 15
Creekmouth. *G Lon* 3C 19
Crews Hill. *G Lon* 1B 18
Cricket Hill. *Hants* 2A 24
Cricklewood. *G Lon* 3A 18
Cripp's Corner. *E Sus* 3B 38
Crockenhill. *Kent* 2D 27
Crocker End. *Oxon* 3D 15
Crockerhill. *Hants* 2B 42
Crockham Hill. *Kent* 3C 27
Crockhurst Street. *Kent* 1A 38
Crockleford Heath. *Essx* 2A 12
Cromer. *Herts* 2A 8
Crondall. *Hants* 1D 33
Crookham. *W Ber* 2B 22
Crookham Village. *Hants* 3D 23
Cross-at-Hand. *Kent* 1B 38
Crossbush. *W Sus* 2C 45
Cross End. *Essx* 1C 11
Cross in Hand. *E Sus* 3D 37
Crouch. *Kent* 3A 28
Croughton. *Nptn* 1B 4
Crowborough. *E Sus* 2D 37
Crowdhill. *Hants* 1A 42
Crowfield. *Nptn* 1C 5
Crow Green. *Essx* 2D 19
Crowhurst. *E Sus* 1B 48
Crowhurst. *Surr* 1B 36
Crowhurst Lane End. *Surr* 1B 36
Crowmarsh Gifford. *Oxon* 3C 15
Crowthorne. *Brac* 2A 24
Croxley Green. *Herts* 2C 17
Croydon. *G Lon* 2B 26
Crundale. *Kent* 1A 40
Crux Easton. *Hants* 3A 22
Cryers Hill. *Buck* 2A 16
Crystal Palace. *G Lon* 1B 26
Cublington. *Buck* 2A 6
Cuckfield. *W Sus* 3B 36

Cuddesdon. *Oxon* 1C 15
Cuddington. *Buck* 3D 5
Cudham. *G Lon* 3C 27
Cudworth. *Surr* 1A 36
Cuffley. *Herts* 1B 18
Culham. *Oxon* 2B 14
Culverstone Green. *Kent* 2A 28
Cumberlow Green. *Herts* 1B 8
Cumnor. *Oxon* 1A 14
Cupernham. *Hants* 3A 32
Curbridge. *Hants* 1B 42
Curdridge. *Hants* 1B 42
Curridge. *W Ber* 1A 22
Curtisden Green. *Kent* 1B 38
Cutlers Green. *Essx* 1D 9
Cuxham. *Oxon* 2C 15
Cuxton. *Medw* 2B 28

D

Dadford. *Buck* 1C 5
Dagenham. *G Lon* 3C 19
Dagnall. *Buck* 3B 6
Dallington. *E Sus* 1A 48
Danaway. *Kent* 2C 29
Danbury. *Essx* 1B 20
Dane End. *Herts* 2B 8
Danehill. *E Sus* 3C 37
Daneshill. *Hants* 3C 23
Daniel's Water. *Kent* 1D 39
Darenth. *Kent* 1D 27
Dargate. *Kent* 2A 30
Dartford. *Kent* 1D 27
Dartford-Thurrock River Crossing.
Kent 1D 27
Dassels. *Herts* 2B 8
Datchet. *Wind* 1B 24
Datchworth. *Herts* 3A 8
Datchworth Green. *Herts* 3A 8
Dawesgreen. *Surr* 1A 36
Daws Heath. *Essx* 3C 21
Deadman's Cross. *C Beds* 1D 7
Deal. *Kent* 3D 31
Dean. *Hants* 1B 42
(nr. Bishop's Waltham)
Dean. *Hants* 2A 32
(nr. Winchester)
Deane. *Hants* 3B 22
Deanlane End. *W Sus* 1D 43
Deanshanger. *Nptn* 1D 5
Debden. *Essx* 1D 9
Debden Green. *Essx* 2C 19
(nr. Loughton)
Debden Green. *Essx* 1D 9
(nr. Saffron Walden)
Deddington. *Oxon* 1A 4
Dedham. *Essx* 1A 12
Dedham Heath. *Essx* 1A 12
Deepcut. *Surr* 3B 24
Delly End. *Oxon* 3A 4
Delvin End. *Essx* 1B 10
Denchworth. *Oxon* 2A 14
Dengie. *Essx* 1D 21
Denham. *Buck* 3C 17
Denham Green. *Buck* 3C 17
Denmead. *Hants* 1C 43
Densole. *Kent* 1C 41
Denstroude. *Kent* 2B 30
Denton. *E Sus* 2C 47
Denton. *Kent* 1C 41
Denton. *Oxon* 1B 14
Deptford. *G Lon* 1B 26
Derringstone. *Kent* 1C 41
Detling. *Kent* 3B 28
Dial Green. *W Sus* 3A 34
Dial Post. *W Sus* 1D 45
Dibden. *Hants* 2A 42
Dibden Purlieu. *Hants* 2A 42
Didcot. *Oxon* 2B 14
Didling. *W Sus* 1A 44
Digswell. *Herts* 3A 8
Dingleden. *Kent* 2C 39
Dinton. *Buck* 3D 5
Dipley. *Hants* 3D 23
Dippenhall. *Surr* 1A 34
Ditchling. *E Sus* 1B 46
Ditton. *Kent* 3B 28
Doddinghurst. *Essx* 2D 19
Doddington. *Kent* 3D 29
Dogmersfield. *Hants* 3D 23
Donkey Street. *Kent* 2B 40
Donkey Town. *Surr* 2B 24
Donnington. *W Ber* 2A 22
Donnington. *W Sus* 2A 44
Doomsday Green. *W Sus* 2D 35
Dorchester on Thames. *Oxon* 2C 15
Dorking. *Surr* 1D 35
Dorking Tye. *Suff* 1D 11
Dormansland. *Surr* 1C 37
Dormans Park. *Surr* 1B 36
Dorney. *Buck* 1B 24
Dorton. *Buck* 3C 5
Dover. *Kent* ....1D 41 & **51**
Dovercourt. *Essx* 1C 13
Doversgreen. *Surr* 1A 36
Dowlesgreen. *Wok* 2A 24

Downe. G Lon 2C 27
Downend. IOW 3B 42
Downend. W Ber 1A 22
Downham. Essx 2B 20
Downley. Buck 2A 16
Downside. Surr 3D 25
Dragons Green. W Sus 3D 35
Draycot. Oxon 1C 15
Drayton. Oxon ....2A 14 (nr. Abingdon)
Drayton. Oxon ....1A 4 (nr. Banbury)
Drayton. Port 2C 43
Drayton Beauchamp. Buck 3B 6
Drayton Parslow. Buck 2A 6
Drayton St Leonard. Oxon 2B 14
Drellingore. Kent 1C 41
Droxford. Hants 1C 43
Dry Sandford. Oxon 1A 14
Dry Street. Essx 3A 20
Duck End. Essx 2A 10
Ducklington. Oxon 1A 14
Duddenhoe End. Essx 1C 9
Duddleswell. E Sus 3C 37
Dulwich. G Lon 1B 26
Dummer. Hants 1B 32
Dumpford. W Sus 3A 34
Duncton. W Sus 1B 44
Dundridge. Hants 1B 42
Dungate. Kent 3D 29
Dungeness. Kent 3A 40
Dunkirk. Kent 3A 30
Dunk's Green. Kent 3A 28
Dunley. Hants 3A 22
Dunsden Green. Oxon 1D 23
Dunsfold. Surr 2C 35
Dunsmore. Buck 1A 16
Dunstable. C Beds 2C 7
Duns Tew. Oxon 2A 4
Dunton. Buck 2A 6
Dunton Green. Kent 3D 27
Durgates. E Sus 2A 38
Durley. Hants 1B 42
Durley Street. Hants 1B 42
Durrant Green. Kent 2C 39
Durrants. Hants 1D 43
Durrington. W Sus 2D 45
Duton Hill. Essx 2A 10
Duxford. Oxon 2A 14
Dymchurch. Kent 3B 40

E

Ealing. G Lon 3D 17
Earley. Wok 1D 23
Earls Colne. Essx 2C 11
Earnley. W Sus 3A 44
Eartham. W Sus 2B 44
Easebourne. W Sus 3A 34
Eashing. Surr 1B 34
Easington. Buck 3C 5
Easington. Oxon ....1A 4 (nr. Banbury)
Easington. Oxon ....2C 15 (nr. Watlington)
Easole Street. Kent 3C 31
East Anton. Hants 1A 32
East Ashling. W Sus 2A 44
East Aston. Hants 1A 32
East Barnet. G Lon 2A 18
East Beach. W Sus 3A 44
East Bedfont. G Lon 1C 25
East Bergholt. Suff 1A 12
East Blatchington. E Sus 2C 47
East Boldre. Hants 2A 42
Eastbourne. E Sus ....3A 48 & 51
East Burnham. Buck 3B 16
Eastbury. Herts 2C 17
Eastbury. W Ber 1A 22
East Challow. Oxon 3A 14
East Chiltington. E Sus 1B 46
Eastchurch. Kent 1D 29
East Clandon. Surr 3C 25
East Claydon. Buck 2D 5
Eastcote. G Lon 3D 17
East Cowes. IOW 3B 42
East Dean. E Sus 3D 47
East Dean. W Sus 1B 44
East End. Hants ....3A 42 (nr. Lymington)
East End. Hants ....2A 22 (nr. Newbury)
East End. Herts 2C 9
East End. Kent ....1D 29 (nr. Minster)
East End. Kent ....2C 9 (nr. Tenterden)
East End. Oxon 3A 4
East End. Suff 1B 12
Eastergate. W Sus 2B 44
East Farleigh. Kent 3B 28
East Garston. W Ber 1A 22
East Ginge. Oxon 3A 14
East Gores. Essx 2C 11
East Grinstead. W Sus 2B 36
East Guldeford. E Sus 3D 39

East Hagbourne. Oxon 3B 14
East Ham. G Lon 3C 19
Easthampstead. Brac 2A 24
East Hanney. Oxon 2A 14
East Hanningfield. Essx 1B 20
East Harting. W Sus 1A 44
East Hendred. Oxon 3A 14
East Hoathly. E Sus 1D 47
Easthorpe. Essx 2D 11
East Horsley. Surr 3C 25
East Hyde. C Beds 3D 7
East Ilsley. W Ber 3A 14
East Langdon. Kent 1D 41
East Lavington. W Sus 1B 44
East Lavant. W Sus 2A 44
Eastleigh. Hants 1A 42
Eastling. Kent 3D 29
East Liss. Hants 3D 33
East Lockinge. Oxon 3A 14
East Malling. Kent 3B 28
East Marden. W Sus 1A 44
East Meon. Hants 3C 33
East Mersea. Essx 3A 12
East Molesey. Surr 2D 25
Eastney. Port 3C 43
East Oakley. Hants 3B 22
Easton. Hants 2B 32
East Peckham. Kent 1A 38
East Preston. W Sus 2C 45
Eastry. Kent 3D 31
East Shefford. W Ber 1A 22
East Stourmouth. Kent 2C 31
East Stratton. Hants 1B 32
East Studdal. Kent 1D 41
East Tilbury. Thur 1A 28
East Tisted. Hants 2D 33
Eastwick. Herts 3C 9
East Wittering. W Sus 3D 43
Eastwood. S'end 3C 21
East Woodhay. Hants 2A 22
East Worldham. Hants 2D 33
Eaton. Oxon 1A 14
Eaton Bray. C Beds 2B 6
Ebbsfleet. Kent 1A 28
Ebernoe. W Sus 3B 34
Ecchinswell. Hants 3B 22
Eccles. Kent 2B 28
Edburton. W Sus 1A 46
Eddington. Kent 2B 30
Eddington. W Ber 2A 22
Edenbridge. Kent 1C 37
Edgcott. Buck 2C 5
Edgware. G Lon 2D 17
Edlesborough. Buck 3B 6
Edmonton. G Lon 2B 18
Edney Common. Essx 1A 20
Edwardstone. Suff 1D 11
Edworth. C Beds 1A 8
Effingham. Surr 3D 25
Effingham Common. Surr 3D 25
Egbury. Hants 3A 22
Egerton. Kent 1D 39
Egerton Forstal. Kent 1C 39
Eggington. C Beds 2B 6
Egham. Surr 1C 25
Egham Hythe. Surr 1C 25
Egypt. Buck 3B 16
Egypt. Hants 1A 32
Eight Ash Green. Essx 2D 11
Elbridge. W Sus 2B 44
Elcot. W Ber 2A 22
Elder Street. Essx 1D 9
Elham. Kent 1B 40
Eling. Hants 1A 42
Eling. W Ber 1B 22
Elkins Green. Essx 1A 20
Ellenbrook. Herts 1A 18
Ellen's Green. Surr 2C 35
Ellesborough. Buck 1A 16
Ellisfield. Hants 1C 33
Elmdon. Essx 1C 9
Elmfield. IOW 3B 42
Elm Park. G Lon 3D 19
Elmstead. Essx 2A 12
Elmstead Heath. Essx 2A 12
Elmstead Market. Essx 2A 12
Elmsted. Kent 1B 40
Elmstone. Kent 2C 31
Elsenham. Essx 2D 9
Elsfield. Oxon 3B 4
Elstead. Surr 1B 34
Elsted. W Sus 1A 44
Elsted Marsh. W Sus 3A 34
Elstree. Herts 2D 17
Eltham. G Lon 1C 27
Elvetham Heath. Hants 3D 23
Elvington. Kent 3C 31
Emmbrook. Wok 2D 23
Emmer Green. Read 1D 23
Emmington. Oxon 1D 15
Empshott. Hants 2D 33
Emsworth. Hants 2D 43
Enborne. W Ber 2A 22
Enborne Row. W Ber 2A 22
Enfield. G Lon 2B 18
Enfield Wash. G Lon 2B 18

Englefield. W Ber 1C 23
Englefield Green. Surr 1B 24
Enham Alamein. Hants 1A 32
Enstone. Oxon 2A 4
Epping. Essx 1C 19
Epping Green. Essx 1C 19
Epping Green. Herts 1A 18
Epping Upland. Essx 1C 19
Epsom. Surr 2A 26
Epwell. Oxon 1A 4
Eridge Green. E Sus 2D 37
Erith. G Lon 1D 27
Erriottwood. Kent 3D 29
Erwarton. Suff 1C 13
Essendon. Herts 1A 18
Etchingham. E Sus 3B 38
Etchinghill. Kent 2B 40
Eton. Wind 1B 24
Eton Wick. Wind 1B 24
Evenley. Nptn 1B 4
Eversholt. C Beds 1B 6
Eversley. Hants 2D 23
Eversley Centre. Hants 2D 23
Eversley Cross. Hants 2D 23
Ewell. Surr 2A 26
Ewell Minnis. Kent 1C 41
Ewelme. Oxon 2C 15
Ewhurst. Surr 1C 35
Ewhurst Green. E Sus 3B 38
Ewhurst Green. Surr 2C 35
Ewshot. Hants 3A 24
Exbury. Hants 2A 42
Exceat. E Sus 3D 47
Exlade Street. Oxon 3C 15
Exton. Hants 3C 33
Eyhorne Street. Kent 3C 29
Eynsford. Kent 2D 27
Eynsham. Oxon 1A 14
Eythorne. Kent 1C 41

F

Faccombe. Hants 3A 22
Fairbourne Heath. Kent 3C 29
Fairhill. Kent 3D 39
Fairlands. Surr 3B 24
Fairlight. E Sus 1C 49
Fairlight Cove. E Sus 1C 49
Fairmile. Surr 2D 25
Fair Oak. Hants ....1A 42 (nr. Eastleigh)
Fair Oak. Hants ....2B 22 (nr. Kingsclere)
Fair Oak Green. Hants 2C 23
Fairseat. Kent 2A 28
Fairstead. Essx 3B 10
Fairwarp. E Sus 3C 37
Falkenham. Suff 1C 13
Falmer. E Sus 2B 46
Fancott. C Beds 2C 7
Fanner's Green. Essx 3A 10
Fareham. Hants 2B 42
Farleigh. Surr 2B 26
Farleigh Wallop. Hants 1C 33
Farley Green. Surr 1C 35
Farley Hill. Wok 2D 23
Farlington. Port 2C 43
Farmoor. Oxon 1A 14
Farnborough. G Lon 2C 27
Farnborough. Hants 3A 24
Farnborough. W Ber 3A 14
Farncombe. Surr 1B 34
Farnham. Essx 2C 9
Farnham. Surr 1A 34
Farnham Common. Buck 3B 16
Farnham Green. Essx 2C 9
Farnham Royal. Buck 3B 16
Farningham. Kent 2D 27
Farthinghoe. Nptn 1B 4
Faulkbourne. Essx 3B 10
Faversham. Kent 2D 30
Fawkham Green. Kent 2D 27
Fawler. Oxon 3A 4
Fawley. Buck 3D 15
Fawley. Hants 2A 42
Fawley. W Ber 3A 14
Faygate. W Sus 2A 36
Feering. Essx 2C 11
Felbridge. Surr 2B 36
Felcourt. Surr 1B 36
Felden. Herts 1C 17
Felixstowe. Suff 1C 13
Felixstowe Ferry. Suff 1D 13
Felpham. W Sus 3B 44
Felsted. Essx 3A 10
Feltham. G Lon 1D 25
Felthamhill. Surr 1D 25
Fencott. Oxon 3B 4
Fenn Street. Medw 1B 28
Fenny Stratford. Mil 1A 6
Fernhill. W Sus 1A 36
Fernhurst. W Sus 3A 34
Ferring. W Sus 2D 45
Fetcham. Surr 3D 25
Fewcott. Oxon 2B 4

Fiddlers Hamlet. Essx 1C 19
Fifield. Wind 1B 24
Finchampstead. Wok 2D 23
Finchdean. Hants 1D 43
Finchingfield. Essx 1A 10
Finchley. G Lon 2A 18
Findon. W Sus 2D 45
Findon Valley. W Sus 2D 45
Fingest. Buck 2D 15
Finglesham. Kent 3D 31
Fingringhoe. Essx 2A 12
Finmere. Oxon 1C 5
Finsbury. G Lon 3B 18
Finstock. Oxon 3A 4
Firle. E Sus 2C 47
Fishbourne. IOW 3B 42
Fishbourne. W Sus 2B 44
Fisher's Pond. Hants 3A 32
Fisherstreet. W Sus 2B 34
Fittleworth. W Sus 1C 45
Five Ash Down. E Sus 3C 37
Five Ashes. E Sus 3D 37
Five Oak Green. Kent 1A 38
Five Oaks. W Sus 3C 35
Flack's Green. Essx 3B 10
Flackwell Heath. Buck 3A 16
Flamstead. Herts 3C 7
Flansham. W Sus 2B 44
Flaunden. Herts 1C 17
Fleet. Hants ....3A 24 (nr. Farnborough)
Fleet. Hants ....2D 43 (nr. South Hayling)
Fleetville. Herts 1D 17
Fletcher's Green. Kent 1D 37
Fletching. E Sus 3C 37
Flexford. Surr 3B 24
Flimwell. E Sus 2B 38
Flishinghurst. Kent 2B 38
Flitton. C Beds 1C 7
Flitwick. C Beds 1C 7
Fobbing. Thur 3B 20
Folkestone. Kent ....2C 41 & 56
Folkington. E Sus 2D 47
Folly, The. Herts 3D 7
Folly, The. W Ber 2A 22
Fontwell. W Sus 2B 44
Foots Cray. G Lon 1C 27
Ford. Buck 1D 15
Ford. W Sus 2C 45
Fordcombe. Kent 1D 37
Ford End. Essx 3A 10
Fordham. Essx 2D 11
Fordham Heath. Essx 2D 11
Ford Street. Essx 2D 11
Fordwich. Kent 3B 30
Forest Green. Surr 1D 35
Forest Hill. Oxon 1B 14
Forest Row. E Sus 2C 37
Forestside. W Sus 1D 43
Forstal, The. Kent 2A 40
Forton. Hants 1A 32
Forty Green. Buck 2B 16
Forty Hill. G Lon 2B 18
Foster Street. Essx 1C 19
Foul Mile. E Sus 1A 48
Four Elms. Kent 1C 37
Four Marks. Hants 2C 33
Four Oaks. E Sus 3C 39
Four Throws. Kent 3B 38
Foxcombe Hill. Oxon 1A 14
Fox Corner. Surr 3B 24
Fox Hatch. Essx 2D 19
Foxhunt Green. E Sus 1D 47
Fox Lane. Hants 3A 24
Fox Street. Essx 2D 11
Framfield. E Sus 3C 37
Frant. E Sus 2D 37
Frating Green. Essx 2A 12
Fratton. Port 2C 43
Freefolk Priors. Hants 1A 32
Freeland. Oxon 3A 4
French Street. Kent 3C 27
Frensham. Surr 1A 34
Freshwater. IOW 3A 42
Freston. Suff 1B 12
Friar's Gate. E Sus 2C 37
Friday Street. E Sus 2A 48
Friday Street. Surr 1D 35
Friern Barnet. G Lon 2A 18
Frieth. Buck 2D 15
Frilford. Oxon 2A 14
Frilsham. W Ber 1B 22
Frimley. Surr 3A 24
Frimley Green. Surr 3A 24
Frindsbury. Medw 2B 28
Fringford. Oxon 2C 5
Frinsted. Kent 3C 29
Frinton-on-Sea. Essx 3C 13
Friston. E Sus 3D 47
Frithsden. Herts 1C 17
Frittenden. Kent 1C 39
Fritwell. Oxon 2B 4
Frogham. Kent 3C 31
Frogmore. Hants 2A 24
Frogmore. Herts 1D 17
Froxfield. C Beds 1B 6

Froxfield Green—Heston

Froxfield Green. *Hants* 3D **33**
Fryern Hill. *Hants* 3A **32**
Fryerning. *Essx* 1A **20**
Fulflood. *Hants* 2A **32**
Fulham. *G Lon* 1A **26**
Fulking. *W Sus* 1A **46**
Fuller Street. *Essx* 3B **10**
Fullerton. *Hants* 2A **32**
Fulmer. *Buck* 3B **16**
Funtington. *W Sus* 2A **44**
Funtley. *Hants* 2B **42**
Furner's Green. *E Sus* 3C **37**
Furneux Pelham. *Herts* 2C **9**
Furzeley Corner. *Hants* 1C **43**
Furzey Lodge. *Hants* 2A **42**
Fyfield. *Essx* 1D **19**
Fyfield. *Oxon* 2A **14**
Fyning. *W Sus* 3A **34**

G

Gadbrook. *Surr* 1A **36**
Gagingwell. *Oxon* 2A **4**
Gainsborough. *Suff* 1B **12**
Gainsford End. *Essx* 1B **10**
Galleyend. *Essx* 1B **20**
Galleywood. *Essx* 1B **20**
Gallowstree Common. *Oxon* 3C **15**
Gants Hill. *G Lon* 3C **19**
Gardeners Green. *Wok* 2A **24**
Garford. *Oxon* 2A **14**
Garlinge Green. *Kent* 3B **30**
Garsington. *Oxon* 1B **14**
Gatton. *Surr* 3A **26**
Gatwick (London) Airport. *W Sus* 1A **36** & **58**
Gawcott. *Buck* 1C **5**
Gay Bowers. *Essx* 1B **20**
Gay Street. *W Sus* 3C **35**
George Green. *Buck* 3B **16**
Gerrards Cross. *Buck* 3B **16**
Gestingthorpe. *Essx* 1C **11**
Gibraltar. *Buck* 3D **5**
Gidea Park. *G Lon* 3D **19**
Gillingham. *Medw* 2B **28** & **Medway 54**
Gill's Green. *Kent* 2B **38**
Glassenbury. *Kent* 2B **38**
Glympton. *Oxon* 2A **4**
Glynde. *E Sus* 2C **47**
Glyndebourne. *E Sus* 1C **47**
Goathurst Common. *Kent* 3C **27**
Goat Lees. *Kent* 1A **40**
Godalming. *Surr* 1B **34**
Goddard's Green. *Kent* 2C **39** (nr. Benenden)
Goddard's Green. *Kent* 2B **38** (nr. Cranbrook)
Goddards Green. *W Sus* 3A **36**
Godmersham. *Kent* 3A **30**
Godstone. *Surr* 3B **26**
Goff's Oak. *Herts* 1B **18**
Golden Cross. *E Sus* 1D **47**
Golden Green. *Kent* 1A **38**
Golden Pot. *Hants* 1D **33**
Golders Green. *G Lon* 3A **18**
Goldhanger. *Essx* 1D **21**
Goldstone. *Kent* 2C **31**
Gomshall. *Surr* 1C **35**
Good Easter. *Essx* 3A **10**
Goodmayes. *G Lon* 3C **19**
Goodnestone. *Kent* 3C **31** (nr. Aylesham)
Goodnestone. *Kent* 2A **30** (nr. Faversham)
Goodworth Clatford. *Hants* 1A **32**
Goosey. *Oxon* 2A **14**
Goring. *Oxon* 3C **15**
Goring-by-Sea. *W Sus* 2D **45**
Goring Heath. *Oxon* 1C **23**
Gosfield. *Essx* 2B **10**
Gosford. *Oxon* 3B **4**
Gosmore. *Herts* 2D **7**
Gosport. *Hants* 2C **43**
Gossops Green. *W Sus* 2A **36**
Goudhurst. *Kent* 2B **38**
Graffham. *W Sus* 1B **44**
Grafham. *Surr* 1C **35**
Grafty Green. *Kent* 1C **39**
Grain. *Medw* 1C **29**
Granborough. *Buck* 2D **5**
Grandpont. *Oxon* 1B **14**
Grange Hill. *G Lon* 2C **19**
Graveley. *Herts* 2A **8**
Graveney. *Kent* 2A **30**
Gravesend. *Kent* 1A **28**
Grays. *Thur* 1A **28**
Grayshott. *Hants* 2A **34**
Grayswood. *Surr* 2B **34**
Grazeley. *Wok* 2C **23**
Great Amwell. *Herts* 3B **8**
Great Baddow. *Essx* 1B **20**
Great Bardfield. *Essx* 1A **10**
Great Bentley. *Essx* 2B **12**
Great Bookham. *Surr* 3D **25**
Great Braxted. *Essx* 3C **11**
Great Brickhill. *Buck* 1B **6**
Great Bromley. *Essx* 2A **12**
Great Burstead. *Essx* 2A **20**
Great Canfield. *Essx* 3D **9**
Great Chart. *Kent* 1D **39**
Great Chesterford. *Essx* 1D **9**
Great Chishill. *Cambs* 1C **9**
Great Clacton. *Essx* 3B **12**
Great Cornard. *Suff* 1C **11**
Great Dunmow. *Essx* 2A **10**
Great Easton. *Essx* 2A **10**
Great Gaddesden. *Herts* 3C **7**
Great Hallingbury. *Essx* 3D **9**
Greatham. *Hants* 2D **33**
Greatham. *W Sus* 1C **45**
Great Hampden. *Buck* 1A **16**
Great Haseley. *Oxon* 1C **15**
Great Henny. *Essx* 1C **11**
Great Holland. *Essx* 3C **13**
Great Horkesley. *Essx* 1D **11**
Great Hormead. *Herts* 1C **9**
Great Horwood. *Buck* 1D **5**
Great Kimble. *Buck* 1A **16**
Great Kingshill. *Buck* 2A **16**
Great Leighs. *Essx* 3B **10**
Great Linford. *Mil* 1A **6**
Great Maplestead. *Essx* 1C **11**
Great Milton. *Oxon* 1C **15**
Great Missenden. *Buck* 1A **16**
Great Mongeham. *Kent* 3D **31**
Great Munden. *Herts* 2B **8**
Great Notley. *Essx* 2B **10**
Great Oakley. *Essx* 2B **12**
Great Offley. *Herts* 2D **7**
Great Oxney Green. *Essx* 1A **20**
Great Parndon. *Essx* 1C **19**
Great Saling. *Essx* 2A **10**
Great Sampford. *Essx* 1A **10**
Great Shefford. *W Ber* 1A **22**
Great Stambridge. *Essx* 2C **21**
Great Stonar. *Kent* 3D **31**
Greatstone-on-Sea. *Kent* 3A **40**
Great Tew. *Oxon* 2A **4**
Great Tey. *Essx* 2C **11**
Great Thorness. *IOW* 3A **42**
Great Totham North. *Essx* 3C **11**
Great Totham South. *Essx* 3C **11**
Great Wakering. *Essx* 3D **21**
Great Waldingfield. *Suff* 1D **11**
Great Waltham. *Essx* 3A **10**
Great Warley. *Essx* 2D **19**
Great Wenham. *Suff* 1A **12**
Great Wigborough. *Essx* 3D **11**
Greatworth. *Nptn* 1B **4**
Great Wymondley. *Herts* 2A **8**
Great Yeldham. *Essx* 1B **10**
Green End. *Herts* 1B **8** (nr. Buntingford)
Green End. *Herts* 2B **8** (nr. Stevenage)
Greenfield. *C Beds* 1C **7**
Greenfield. *Oxon* 2D **15**
Greenford. *G Lon* 3D **17**
Greenham. *W Ber* 2A **22**
Greenhill. *Kent* 2B **30**
Greenhithe. *Kent* 1D **27**
Greenstead Green. *Essx* 2C **11**
Greensted Green. *Essx* 1D **19**
Green Street. *Herts* 2D **17**
Green Street Green. *G Lon* 2C **27**
Green Street Green. *Kent* 1D **27**
Green Tye. *Herts* 3C **9**
Greenwich. *G Lon* 1B **26**
Grendon Underwood. *Buck* 2C **5**
Greywell. *Hants* 3D **23**
Griggs Green. *Hants* 2A **34**
Grimsbury. *Oxon* 1A **4**
Grisling Common. *E Sus* 3C **37**
Groombridge. *E Sus* 2D **37**
Groton. *Suff* 1D **11**
Grove. *Kent* 2C **31**
Grove. *Oxon* 2A **14**
Grove Park. *G Lon* 1C **27**
Gubblecote. *Herts* 3B **6**
Guestling Green. *E Sus* 1C **49**
Guestling Thorn. *E Sus* 1C **49**
Guildford. *Surr* 1B **34** & **54**
Gundleton. *Hants* 2C **33**
Gun Green. *Kent* 2B **38**
Gun Hill. *E Sus* 1D **47**
Gunville. *IOW* 3A **42**
Gurnard. *IOW* 3A **42**
Guston. *Kent* 1D **41**

H

Habin. *W Sus* 3A **34**
Hackney. *G Lon* 3B **18**
Haddenham. *Buck* 1D **15**
Hadham Cross. *Herts* 3C **9**
Hadham Ford. *Herts* 2C **9**
Hadleigh. *Essx* 3C **21**
Hadleigh. *Suff* 1A **12**
Hadleigh Heath. *Suff* 1D **11**
Hadley Wood. *G Lon* 2A **18**
Hadlow. *Kent* 1A **38**
Hadlow Down. *E Sus* 3D **37**
Haffenden Quarter. *Kent* 1C **39**
Hailey. *Herts* 3B **8**
Hailey. *Oxon* 3A **4**
Hailsham. *E Sus* 2D **47**
Hainault. *G Lon* 2C **19**
Hale. *Surr* 1A **34**
Hale Street. *Kent* 1A **38**
Halfway. *W Ber* 2A **22**
Halfway Houses. *Kent* 1D **29**
Halland. *E Sus* 1D **47**
Halling. *Medw* 2B **28**
Hall's Green. *Herts* 2A **8**
Halnaker. *W Sus* 2B **44**
Halse. *Nptn* 1B **4**
Halstead. *Essx* 1C **11**
Halstead. *Kent* 2C **27**
Halton. *Buck* 1A **16**
Ham. *G Lon* 1D **25**
Ham. *Kent* 3D **31**
Hambleden. *Buck* 3D **15**
Hambledon. *Hants* 1C **43**
Hambledon. *Surr* 2B **34**
Hamble-le-Rice. *Hants* 2A **42**
Hambrook. *W Sus* 2D **43**
Ham Green. *Kent* 2C **29**
Ham Hill. *Kent* 2A **28**
Hammer. *W Sus* 2A **34**
Hammersmith. *G Lon* 1A **26**
Hammerwood. *E Sus* 2C **37**
Hammill. *Kent* 3C **31**
Hammond Street. *Herts* 1B **18**
Hampden Park. *E Sus* 2A **48**
Hamperden End. *Essx* 1D **9**
Hampstead. *G Lon* 3A **18**
Hampstead Norreys. *W Ber* 1B **22**
Hampton. *G Lon* 1D **25**
Hampton. *Kent* 2B **30**
Hampton Poyle. *Oxon* 3B **4**
Hampton Wick. *G Lon* 2D **25**
Hamsey. *E Sus* 1C **47**
Hamsey Green. *Surr* 3B **26**
Hamstead. *IOW* 3A **42**
Hamstead Marshall. *W Ber* 2A **22**
Hamstreet. *Kent* 2A **40**
Handcross. *W Sus* 3A **36**
Handy Cross. *Buck* 2A **16**
Hangleton. *Brig* 2A **46**
Hangleton. *W Sus* 2C **45**
Hankham. *E Sus* 2A **48**
Hannington. *Hants* 3B **22**
Hanscombe End. *C Beds* 1D **7**
Hanwell. *G Lon* 3D **17**
Hanwell. *Oxon* 1A **4**
Hanworth. *G Lon* 1D **25**
Harbledown. *Kent* 3B **30**
Hardham. *W Sus* 1C **45**
Hardley. *Hants* 2A **42**
Hardway. *Hants* 2C **43**
Hardwick. *Buck* 3A **6**
Hardwick. *Oxon* 2B **4** (nr. Bicester)
Hardwick. *Oxon* 1A **14** (nr. Witney)
Hardy's Green. *Essx* 2D **11**
Harefield. *G Lon* 2C **17**
Hare Green. *Essx* 2A **12**
Hare Hatch. *Wok* 1A **24**
Hareplain. *Kent* 2C **39**
Hare Street. *Essx* 1C **19**
Hare Street. *Herts* 2B **8**
Harkstead. *Suff* 1B **12**
Harlington. *C Beds* 1C **7**
Harlington. *G Lon* 1C **25**
Harlow. *Essx* 3C **9**
Harmer Green. *Herts* 3A **8**
Harmondsworth. *G Lon* 1C **25**
Harold Hill. *G Lon* 2D **19**
Harold Wood. *G Lon* 2D **19**
Harpenden. *Herts* 3D **7**
Harpsden. *Oxon* 3D **15**
Harrietsham. *Kent* 3C **29**
Harrow. *G Lon* 3D **17**
Harrow on the Hill. *G Lon* 3D **17**
Harrow Weald. *G Lon* 2D **17**
Hartfield. *E Sus* 2C **37**
Hartfordbridge. *Hants* 3D **23**
Hartford End. *Essx* 3A **10**
Hartley. *Kent* 2B **38** (nr. Cranbrook)
Hartley. *Kent* 2A **28** (nr. Dartford)
Hartley Mauditt. *Hants* 2D **33**
Hartley Wespall. *Hants* 3C **23**
Hartley Wintney. *Hants* 3D **23**
Hartlip. *Kent* 2C **29**
Harvel. *Kent* 2A **28**
Harwell. *Oxon* 3A **14**
Harwich. *Essx* 1C **13**
Hascombe. *Surr* 2B **34**
Haslemere. *Surr* 2B **34**
Hassell Street. *Kent* 1A **40**
Hassocks. *W Sus* 1B **46**
Hastingleigh. *Kent* 1A **40**
Hastings. *E Sus* 2C **49**
Hastingwood. *Essx* 1C **19**
Hastoe. *Herts* 1B **16**
Hatch End. *G Lon* 2D **17**
Hatching Green. *Herts* 3D **7**
Hatch Warren. *Hants* 1C **33**
Hatfield. *Herts* 1A **18**
Hatfield Broad Oak. *Essx* 3D **9**
Hatfield Garden Village. *Herts* 1A **18**
Hatfield Heath. *Essx* 3D **9**
Hatfield Hyde. *Herts* 3A **8**
Hatfield Peverel. *Essx* 3B **10**
Hatherden. *Hants* 3A **22**
Hattingley. *Hants* 2C **33**
Hatton. *G Lon* 1C **25**
Haultwick. *Herts* 2B **8**
Havant. *Hants* 2D **43**
Havenstreet. *IOW* 3B **42**
Haven, The. *W Sus* 2C **35**
Havering-atte-Bower. *G Lon* 2D **19**
Havering's Grove. *Essx* 2A **20**
Haversham. *Mil* 1A **6**
Hawkenbury. *Kent* 1C **39**
Hawkhurst. *Kent* 2B **38**
Hawkhurst Common. *E Sus* 1D **47**
Hawkinge. *Kent* 1C **41**
Hawkley. *Hants* 3D **33**
Hawkwell. *Essx* 2C **21**
Hawley. *Hants* 3A **24**
Hawley. *Kent* 1D **27**
Hawthorn Hill. *Brac* 1A **24**
Hayes. *G Lon* 2C **27** (nr. Bromley)
Hayes. *G Lon* 3C **17** (nr. Uxbridge)
Haylands. *IOW* 3B **42**
Hayling Island. *Hants* 3D **43**
Haynes. *C Beds* 1C **7**
Haynes West End. *C Beds* 1C **7**
Haysden. *Kent* 1D **37**
Hay Street. *Herts* 2B **8**
Haywards Heath. *W Sus* 3B **36**
Hazeleigh. *Essx* 1C **21**
Hazeley. *Hants* 3D **23**
Hazel Street. *Kent* 2A **38**
Hazlemere. *Buck* 2A **16**
Headbourne Worthy. *Hants* 2A **32**
Headcorn. *Kent* 1C **39**
Headington. *Oxon* 1B **14**
Headley. *Hants* 2A **34** (nr. Haslemere)
Headley. *Hants* 2B **22** (nr. Kingsclere)
Headley. *Surr* 3A **26**
Headley Down. *Hants* 2A **34**
Heath and Reach. *C Beds* 2B **6**
Heath Common. *W Sus* 1D **45**
Heath End. *Hants* 2B **22**
Heathfield. *E Sus* 3D **37**
Heathrow (London) Airport. *G Lon* 1C **25** & **58**
Heath, The. *Suff* 1B **12**
Heaverham. *Kent* 3D **27**
Hebing End. *Herts* 2B **8**
Heckfield. *Hants* 2D **23**
Heckfordbridge. *Essx* 2D **11**
Hedge End. *Hants* 1A **42**
Hedgerley. *Buck* 3B **16**
Helions Bumpstead. *Essx* 1A **10**
Hellingly. *E Sus* 1D **47**
Helmdon. *Nptn* 1B **4**
Hemel Hempstead. *Herts* 1C **17**
Hemley. *Suff* 1C **13**
Hemp's Green. *Essx* 2D **11**
Hempstead. *Essx* 1A **10**
Hempstead. *Medw* 2B **28**
Hempton. *Oxon* 1A **4**
Hendon. *G Lon* 3A **18**
Henfield. *W Sus* 1A **46**
Henham. *Essx* 2D **9**
Henley. *W Sus* 3A **34**
Henley-on-Thames. *Oxon* 3D **15**
Henley's Down. *E Sus* 1B **48**
Henley Street. *Kent* 2A **28**
Henlow. *C Beds* 1D **7**
Henny Street. *Essx* 1C **11**
Hensting. *Hants* 3A **32**
Henton. *Oxon* 1D **15**
Hermitage. *W Ber* 1B **22**
Hermitage. *W Sus* 2D **43**
Herne. *Kent* 2B **30**
Herne Bay. *Kent* 2B **30**
Herne Common. *Kent* 2B **30**
Herne Pound. *Kent* 3A **28**
Hernhill. *Kent* 2A **30**
Heronden. *Kent* 3C **31**
Herongate. *Essx* 2A **20**
Heronsgate. *Herts* 2C **17**
Heron's Ghyll. *E Sus* 3C **37**
Herriard. *Hants* 1C **33**
Hersden. *Kent* 2C **31**
Hersham. *Surr* 2D **25**
Herstmonceux. *E Sus* 1A **48**
Hertford. *Herts* 3B **8**
Hertford Heath. *Herts* 3B **8**
Hertingfordbury. *Herts* 3B **8**
Heston. *G Lon* 1D **25**

South East England Regional Atlas 65

Hethe. *Oxon* .2B 4
Hever. *Kent* 1C 37
Hextable. *Kent* 1D 27
Hexton. *Herts* .1D 7
Heybridge. *Essx* 2A 20
    (nr. Brentwood)
Heybridge. *Essx* 1C 21
    (nr. Maldon)
Heybridge Basin. *Essx* 1C 21
Heydon. *Cambs* 1C 9
Heyshott. *W Sus* 1A 44
Heythrop. *Oxon* 2A 4
Hickstead. *W Sus* 3A 36
Higham. *Kent* .1B 28
Higham. *Suff* 1A 12
Higham Gobion. *C Beds* 1D 7
Higham Wood. *Kent* 1D 37
High Barnet. *G Lon* 2A 18
High Beech. *Essx* 2C 19
Highbrook. *W Sus* 2B 36
High Brooms. *Kent* 1D 37
Highclere. *Hants* 2A 22
High Cogges. *Oxon* 1A 14
High Cross. *Hants* 3D 33
High Cross. *Herts* 3B 8
High Easter. *Essx* 3A 10
High Garrett. *Essx* 2B 10
Highgate. *G Lon* 3A 18
High Halden. *Kent* 2C 39
High Halstow. *Medw* 1B 28
High Hurstwood. *E Sus* 3C 37
High Laver. *Essx* 1D 19
Highleigh. *W Sus* 3A 44
Highmoor. *Oxon* 3D 15
Highmoor Cross. *Oxon* 3D 15
High Ongar. *Essx* 1D 19
High Roding. *Essx* 3A 10
High Salvington. *W Sus* 2D 45
Highsted. *Kent* 2D 29
Highstreet Green. *Essx* 1B 10
Highstreet Green. *Surr* 2B 34
High Wych. *Herts* 3C 9
High Wycombe. *Buck* 2A 16
Hildenborough. *Kent* 1D 37
Hillborough. *Kent* 2C 31
Hill Brow. *Hants* 3D 33
Hillesden. *Buck* 2C 5
Hill Green. *Essx* 1C 9
Hillgreen. *W Ber* 1A 22
Hill Head. *Hants* 2B 42
Hillingdon. *G Lon* 3C 17
Hill Top. *Hants* 2A 42
Hilsea. *Port* 2C 43
Hiltingbury. *Hants* 3A 32
Hindhead. *Surr* 2A 34
Hintlesham. *Suff* 1A 12
Hinton Ampner. *Hants* 3B 32
Hinton-in-the-Hedges.
    Nptn 1B 4
Hinton Waldrist. *Oxon* 2A 14
Hinxhill. *Kent* .1A 40
Hinxworth. *Herts* 1A 8
Hipley. *Hants* 1C 43
Hitchin. *Herts* 2D 7
Hoaden. *Kent* .3C 31
Hoath. *Kent* 2C 31
Hobbs Cross. *Essx* 2C 19
Hockley. *Essx* 2C 21
Hoddesdon. *Herts* 1B 18
Hodsoll Street. *Kent* 2A 28
Hoe Gate. *Hants* 1C 43
Hogben's Hill. *Kent* 3A 30
Hoggeston. *Buck* 2A 6
Holborn. *G Lon* 3B 18
Holbrook. *Suff* .1B 12
Holbury. *Hants* 2A 42
Holder's Green. *Essx* 2A 10
Hole Street. *W Sus* 1D 45
Holland-on-Sea. *Essx* 3C 13
Hollingbourne. *Kent* 3C 29
Hollingbury. *Brig* 2B 46
Hollingdon. *Buck* 2A 6
Hollingrove. *E Sus* 3A 38
Hollington. *E Sus* 1B 48
Holmbury St Mary. *Surr* 1D 35
Holmer Green. *Buck* 2B 16
Holt End. *Hants* 2C 33
Holton. *Oxon* .1C 15
Holton St Mary. *Suff* 1A 12
Holt Pound. *Hants* 1A 34
Holtsmere End. *Herts* 3C 7
Holtye. *E Sus* 2C 37
Holwell. *Herts* .1D 7
Holybourne. *Hants* 1D 33
Holyfield. *Essx* .1B 18
Holyport. *Wind* 1A 24
Honey Hill. *Kent* 2B 30
Honey Tye. *Suff* 1D 11
Honeywick. *C Beds* 2B 6
Hooe. *E Sus* 2A 48
Hooe Common. *E Sus* 1A 48
Hook. *G Lon* 2D 25
Hook. *Hants* 3D 23
    (nr. Basingstoke)
Hook. *Hants* . . . .
    (nr. Fareham)

Hook Green. *Kent* 2A 38
    (nr. Lamberhurst)
Hook Green. *Kent* 1A 28
    (nr. Longfield)
Hook Green. *Kent* 2A 28
    (nr. Meopham)
Hook Norton. *Oxon* 1A 4
Hook's Cross. *Herts* 2A 8
Hookwood. *Surr* 1A 36
Hooley. *Surr* 3A 26
Hoo St Werburgh. *Medw* 1B 28
Hope's Green. *Essx* 3B 20
Horam. *E Sus* .1D 47
Horkesley Heath. *Essx* 2D 11
Horley. *Oxon* .1A 4
Horley. *Surr* 1A 36
Hornchurch. *G Lon* 3D 19
Horndean. *Hants* 1C 43
Horndon on the Hill. *Thur* 3A 20
Horne. *Surr* 1A 36
Horns Corner. *Kent* 3B 38
Horsebridge. *E Sus* 1D 47
Horsebridge. *Hants* 2A 32
Horsell. *Surr* 3B 24
Horsenden. *Buck* 1D 15
Horsham. *W Sus* 2D 35
Horsley Cross. *Essx* 2B 12
Horsleycross Street. *Essx* 2B 12
Horsmonden. *Kent* 1A 38
Horspath. *Oxon* 1B 14
Horsted Keynes. *W Sus* 3B 36
Horton. *Buck* 3B 6
Horton. *Wind* .1C 25
Horton-cum-Studley. *Oxon* 3B 4
Horton Heath. *Hants* 1A 42
Horton Kirby. *Kent* 2D 27
Hothfield. *Kent* 1D 39
Houghton. *W Sus* 1C 45
Houghton Conquest. *C Beds* 1C 7
Houghton Green. *E Sus* 3D 39
Houghton Regis. *C Beds* 2C 7
Hound. *Hants* .2A 42
Hound Green. *Hants* 3D 23
Hounslow. *G Lon* 1D 25
Howe Green. *Essx* 1B 20
    (nr. Chelmsford)
Howegreen. *Essx* 1C 21
    (nr. Maldon)
How End. *C Beds* 1C 7
Howe Street. *Essx* 3A 10
    (nr. Chelmsford)
Howe Street. *Essx* 1A 10
    (nr. Finchingfield)
How Green. *Kent* 1C 37
Howlett End. *Essx* 1D 9
Howt Green. *Kent* 2C 29
Hoyle. *W Sus* 1B 44
Hucking. *Kent* .3C 29
Hughenden Valley. *Buck* 2A 16
Hulcott. *Buck* .3A 6
Hullbridge. *Essx* 2C 21
Hundred Acres. *Hants* 1B 42
Hungerford. *W Ber* 2A 22
Hungerford Newtown. *W Ber* 1A 22
Hunny Hill. *IOW* 3A 42
Hunsdon. *Herts* 3C 9
Hunsdonbury. *Herts* 3C 9
Hunston. *W Sus* 2A 44
Hunters Forstal. *Kent* 2B 30
Hunton. *Hants* 2A 32
Hunton. *Kent* .1B 38
Hunton Bridge. *Herts* 1C 17
Hurley. *Wind* 3A 16
Hursley. *Hants* 3A 32
Hurst. *Wok* 1D 23
Hurstbourne Priors. *Hants* 1A 32
Hurstbourne Tarrant. *Hants* 3A 22
Hurst Green. *Essx* 3B 38
Hurst Green. *Essx* 3A 12
Hurst Green. *Surr* 3B 26
Hurstpierpoint. *W Sus* 1A 46
Hurst Wickham. *W Sus* 1A 46
Hurtmore. *Surr* 1B 34
Husborne Crawley. *C Beds* 1B 6
Hutton. *Essx* 2A 20
Hyde Heath. *Buck* 1B 16
Hydestile. *Surr* .1B 34
Hythe. *Hants* 2A 42
Hythe. *Kent* .2B 40
Hythe End. *Wind* 1C 25

I

Ibstone. *Buck* .2D 15
Ibthorpe. *Hants* 3A 22
Ibworth. *Hants* 3B 22
Ickenham. *G Lon* 3C 17
Ickford. *Buck* 1C 15
Ickham. *Kent* 3C 31
Ickleford. *Herts* 1D 7
Icklesham. *E Sus* 1C 49
Ickleton. *Cambs* 1C 9
Ide Hill. *Kent* 3C 27
Iden. *E Sus* 3D 39

Iden Green. *Kent* 2C 39
    (nr. Benenden)
Iden Green. *Kent* 2B 38
    (nr. Goudhurst)
Iffley. *Oxon* 1B 14
Ifield. *W Sus* 2A 36
Ifieldwood. *W Sus* 2A 36
Ifold. *W Sus* 2C 35
Iford. *E Sus* 2C 47
Ightham. *Kent* .3D 27
Ilford. *G Lon* .3C 19
Ilmer. *Buck* 1D 15
Ingatestone. *Essx* 2A 20
Ingrave. *Essx* 2A 20
Inkpen. *W Ber* .2A 22
Inworth. *Essx* 3C 11
Iping. *W Sus* 3A 34
Ipsden. *Oxon* .3C 15
Ipswich. *Suff* 1B 12
Isfield. *E Sus* 1C 47
Isle of Thanet. *Kent* 2D 31
Isleworth. *G Lon* 1D 25
Islington. *G Lon* 3B 18
Islip. *Oxon* 3B 4
Istead Rise. *Kent* 2A 28
Itchen. *Sotn* 1A 42
Itchen Abbas. *Hants* 2B 32
Itchen Stoke. *Hants* 2B 32
Itchingfield. *W Sus* 3D 35
Iver. *Buck* 3C 17
Iver Heath. *Buck* 3C 17
Ivinghoe. *Buck* .3B 6
Ivinghoe Aston. *Buck* 3B 6
Ivychurch. *Kent* 3A 40
Ivy Hatch. *Kent* 3D 27
Iwade. *Kent* 2D 29

J

Jacobswell. *Surr* 3B 24
Jarvis Brook. *E Sus* 3D 37
Jasper's Green. *Essx* 2B 10
Jaywick. *Essx* 3B 12
Jevington. *E Sus* 2D 47
Jockey End. *Herts* 3C 7
John's Cross. *E Sus* 3B 38
Jordans. *Buck* .2B 16
Jury's Gap. *E Sus* 1D 49

K

Kearsney. *Kent* .1C 41
Kelshall. *Herts* .1B 8
Kelvedon. *Essx* 3C 11
Kelvedon Hatch. *Essx* 2D 19
Kempe's Corner. *Kent* 1A 40
Kempshott. *Hants* 3C 23
Kemp Town. *Brig* 2B 46
Kemsing. *Kent* .3C 27
Kemsley. *Kent* .2D 29
Kenardington. *Kent* 2D 39
Kenley. *G Lon* .3B 26
Kennington. *Kent* 1A 40
Kennington. *Oxon* 1B 14
Kensington. *G Lon* 1A 26
Kensworth. *C Beds* 3C 7
Kensworth Common.
    C Beds 3C 7
Kent International Airport.
    Kent 2D 31
Kenton. *G Lon* .3D 17
Kent Street. *E Sus* 1B 48
Kent Street. *Kent* 3A 28
Kent Street. *W Sus* 3A 36
Keston. *G Lon* .2C 27
Kew. *G Lon* 1D 25
Keymer. *W Sus* 1B 46
Key Street. *Kent* 2C 29
Kidbrooke. *G Lon* 1C 27
Kiddington. *Oxon* 2A 4
Kidlington. *Oxon* 3A 4
Kidmore End. *Oxon* 1C 23
Kilburn. *G Lon* .3A 18
Kilmeston. *Hants* 3B 32
Kilndown. *Kent* 2B 38
Kiln Green. *Wind* 1A 24
Kimble Wick. *Buck* 1A 16
Kimpton. *Herts* 3D 7
Kingsash. *Buck* 1A 16
Kingsclere. *Hants* 3B 22
Kingsdown. *Kent* 1D 41
Kingsey. *Buck* .1D 15
Kingsfold. *W Sus* 2D 35
Kingsgate. *Kent* 1D 31
Kings Hill. *Kent* 3A 28
Kings Langley. *Herts* 1C 17
Kingsley. *Hants* 2D 33
Kingsley Green. *W Sus* 2A 34
Kingsnorth. *Kent* 2A 40
Kingsnorth. *Medw* 1C 29
King's Somborne. *Hants* 2A 32
King's Sutton. *Nptn* 1A 4
Kingston. *Kent* .3B 30
Kingston. *W Sus* 2C 45
Kingston Bagpuize. *Oxon* 2A 14

Kingston Blount. *Oxon* 2D 15
Kingston by Sea. *W Sus* 2A 46
Kingston near Lewes. *E Sus* 2B 46
Kingston Stert. *Oxon* 1D 15
Kingston upon Thames.
    G Lon 2D 25
King's Walden. *Herts* 2D 7
Kingswood. *Buck* 3C 5
Kingswood. *Kent* 3C 29
Kingswood. *Surr* 3A 26
Kings Worthy. *Hants* 2A 32
Kinsbourne Green. *Herts* 3D 7
Kintbury. *W Ber* 2A 22
Kipping's Cross. *Kent* 1A 38
Kirby Cross. *Essx* 2C 13
Kirby-le-Soken. *Essx* 2C 13
Kirdford. *W Sus* 3C 35
Kirtlington. *Oxon* 3B 4
Kirton. *Suff* 1C 13
Kite Hill. *IOW* .3B 42
Kitwood. *Hants* 2C 33
Knaphill. *Surr* 3B 24
Knapp. *Hants* 3A 32
Knatts Valley. *Kent* 2D 27
Knebworth. *Herts* 2A 8
Knockholt. *Kent* 3C 27
Knockholt Pound. *Kent* 3C 27
Knotty Green. *Buck* 2B 16
Knowle Village. *Hants* 2B 42
Knowl Hill. *Wind* 1A 24
Knowlton. *Kent* 3C 31

L

Lacey Green. *Buck* 1A 16
Laddingford. *Kent* 1A 38
Lagness. *W Sus* 2A 44
Laindon. *Essx* 3A 20
Laleham. *Surr* .2C 25
Lamarsh. *Essx* .1C 11
Lamb Corner. *Essx* 1A 12
Lamberhurst. *Kent* 2A 38
Lamberhurst Quarter. *Kent* 2A 38
Lambeth. *G Lon* 1B 26
Lambourne End. *Essx* 2C 19
Lambs Green. *W Sus* 2A 36
Lancing. *W Sus* 2D 45
Landport. *Port* .2C 43
Lane End. *Buck* 2A 16
Lane End. *Hants* 3B 32
Lane End. *IOW* 3C 43
Langdon Hills. *Essx* 3A 20
Langdown. *Hants* 2A 42
Langenhoe. *Essx* 3A 12
Langford. *C Beds* 1D 7
Langford. *Essx* .1C 21
Langham. *Essx* 1A 12
Langley. *Essx* 1C 9
Langley. *Hants* 2A 42
Langley. *Herts* .2A 8
Langley. *Kent* .3C 29
Langley. *Slo* 1C 25
Langley Green. *W Sus* 3A 34
Langleybury. *Herts* 1C 17
Langley Green. *W Sus* 2A 36
Langley Heath. *Kent* 3C 29
Langney. *E Sus* 2A 48
Langrish. *Hants* 3D 33
Langstone. *Hants* 2D 43
Langton Green. *Kent* 2D 37
Larkfield. *Kent* .3A 28
Lasham. *Hants* 1C 33
Lashenden. *Kent* 1C 39
Latchford. *Herts* 2B 8
Latchford. *Oxon* 1C 15
Latchingdon. *Essx* 1C 21
Latchmere Green. *Hants* 2C 23
Latimer. *Buck* .2C 17
Laughton. *E Sus* 1D 47
Launton. *Oxon* 2C 5
Laverstoke. *Hants* 1A 32
Lawford. *Essx* .1A 12
Layer Breton. *Essx* 3D 11
Layer-de-la-Haye. *Essx* 2D 11
Layer Marney. *Essx* 3D 11
Layland's Green. *W Ber* 2A 22
Layter's Green. *Buck* 2B 16
Leaden Roding. *Essx* 3D 9
Leadingcross Green. *Kent* 3C 29
Leagrave. *Lutn* 2C 7
Leatherhead. *Surr* 3D 25
Leaveland. *Kent* 3A 30
Leavenheath. *Suff* 1D 11
Leaves Green. *G Lon* 2C 27
Leckford. *Hants* 2A 32
Leckhampstead. *Buck* 1D 5
Leckhampstead. *W Ber* 1A 22
Leckhampstead Street. *W Ber* 1A 22
Ledburn. *Buck* .2B 6
Ledwell. *Oxon* .2A 4
Lee. *G Lon* 1C 27
Lee. *Hants* 1A 42
Lee Clump. *Buck* 1B 16
Leeds. *Kent* 3C 29
Lee-on-the-Solent. *Hants* 2B 42
Lees, The. *Kent* 3A 30

Lee, The. *Buck* 1B **16**
Leigh. *Kent* 1D **37**
Leigh. *Surr* 1A **36**
Leigh Beck. *Essx* 3C **21**
Leigh Green. *Kent* 2D **39**
Leigh-on-Sea. *S'end* 3C **21**
Leigh Park. *Hants* 2D **43**
Leighton Buzzard. *C Beds* 2B **6**
Lemsford. *Herts* 3A **8**
Lenham. *Kent* 3C **29**
Lenham Heath. *Kent* 1D **39**
Lepe. *Hants* 3A **42**
Letchmore Heath. *Herts* 2D **17**
Letchworth Garden City. *Herts* 1A **8**
Letcombe Bassett. *Oxon* 3A **14**
Letcombe Regis. *Oxon* 3A **14**
Letty Green. *Herts* 3A **8**
Levens Green. *Herts* 2B **8**
Levington. *Suff* 1C **13**
Lewes. *E Sus* 1C **47**
Lewisham. *G Lon* 1B **26**
Lewknor. *Oxon* 2D **15**
Lewson Street. *Kent* 2D **29**
Leybourne. *Kent* 3A **28**
Ley Green. *Herts* 2D **7**
Ley Hill. *Buck* 1B **16**
Leysdown-on-Sea. *Kent* 1A **30**
Leyton. *G Lon* 3B **18**
Leytonstone. *G Lon* 3C **19**
Lickfold. *W Sus* 3B **34**
Lidham Hill. *E Sus* 1C **49**
Lidlington. *C Beds* 1B **6**
Lidsey. *W Sus* 2B **44**
Lidstone. *Oxon* 2A **4**
Lightwater. *Surr* 2B **24**
Lilley. *Herts* 2D **7**
Lillingstone Dayrell. *Buck* 1D **5**
Lillingstone Lovell. *Buck* 1D **5**
Limbury. *Lutn* 2C **7**
Limpsfield. *Surr* 3B **26**
Limpsfield Chart. *Surr* 3C **27**
Linchmere. *W Sus* 2A **34**
Lindfield. *W Sus* 3B **36**
Lindford. *Hants* 2A **34**
Lindsell. *Essx* 2A **10**
Linford. *Thur* 1A **28**
Lingfield. *Surr* 1B **36**
Linkenholt. *Hants* 3A **22**
Linslade. *C Beds* 2B **6**
Linton. *Kent* 3B **28**
Liphook. *Hants* 2A **34**
Lisle Court. *Hants* 3A **42**
Liss. *Hants* 3D **33**
Liss Forest. *Hants* 3D **33**
Litchfield. *Hants* 3A **22**
Litlington. *Cambs* 1B **8**
Litlington. *E Sus* 2D **47**
Little Baddow. *Essx* 1B **20**
Little Bentley. *Essx* 2B **12**
Little Berkhamsted. *Herts* 1A **18**
Little Billington. *C Beds* 2B **6**
Little Bognor. *W Sus* 3C **35**
Little Bookham. *Surr* 3D **25**
Littlebourne. *Kent* 3C **31**
Little Brickhill. *Mil* 1B **6**
Little Bromley. *Essx* 2A **12**
Little Burstead. *Essx* 2A **20**
Littlebury. *Essx* 1D **9**
Littlebury Green. *Essx* 1C **9**
Little Canfield. *Essx* 2D **9**
Little Chalfont. *Buck* 2B **16**
Little Chart. *Kent* 1D **39**
Little Chesterford. *Essx* 1D **9**
Little Chishill. *Cambs* 1C **9**
Little Clacton. *Essx* 3B **12**
Little Common. *E Sus* 2B **48**
Little Cornard. *Suff* 1C **11**
Littlecote. *Buck* 2A **6**
Little Down. *Hants* 3A **22**
Little Dunmow. *Essx* 2A **10**
Little Easton. *Essx* 2A **10**
Little End. *Essx* 1D **19**
Little Gaddesden. *Herts* 3B **6**
Little Hadham. *Herts* 2C **9**
Little Hallingbury. *Essx* 3C **9**
Little Hampden. *Buck* 1A **16**
Littlehampton. *W Sus* 2C **45**
Little Haseley. *Oxon* 1C **15**
Little Horkesley. *Essx* 1D **11**
Little Hormead. *Herts* 2C **9**
Little Horsted. *E Sus* 1C **47**
Little Horwood. *Buck* 1D **5**
Little Kimble. *Buck* 1A **16**
Little Kingshill. *Buck* 2A **16**
Little Laver. *Essx* 1D **19**
Little Leighs. *Essx* 3B **10**
Little London. *Buck* 3C **5**
Little London. *E Sus* 1D **47**
Little London. *Hants* 1A **32**
    (nr. Andover)
Little London. *Hants* 3C **23**
    (nr. Basingstoke)
Little Maplestead. *Essx* 1C **11**
Little Marlow. *Buck* 3A **16**
Little Milton. *Oxon* 1C **15**
Little Missenden. *Buck* 2B **16**

Littlemore. *Oxon* 1B **14**
Little Oakley. *Essx* 2C **13**
Little Posbrook. *Hants* 2B **42**
Little Sampford. *Essx* 1D **9**
Little Sandhurst. *Brac* 2A **24**
Little Somborne. *Hants* 2A **32**
Littlestone-on-Sea. *Kent* 3A **40**
Little Tew. *Oxon* 2A **4**
Little Tey. *Essx* 2C **11**
Little Thurrock. *Thur* 1A **28**
Littleton. *Hants* 2A **32**
Littleton. *Surr* 1B **34**
    (nr. Guildford)
Littleton. *Surr* 2C **25**
    (nr. Staines)
Little Totham. *Essx* 3C **11**
Little Wakering. *Essx* 3D **21**
Little Walden. *Essx* 1D **9**
Little Waltham. *Essx* 3B **10**
Little Warley. *Essx* 2A **20**
Little Wenham. *Suff* 1A **12**
Littlewick Green. *Wind* 1A **24**
Little Wittenham. *Oxon* 2B **14**
Littleworth. *W Sus* 3D **35**
Little Wymondley. *Herts* 2A **8**
Little Yeldham. *Essx* 1B **10**
Littley Green. *Essx* 3A **10**
Locksgreen. *IOW* 3A **42**
Locks Heath. *Hants* 2B **42**
Lodsworth. *W Sus* 3B **34**
London. *G Lon* ....3B **18** & 52-53
London Ashford (Lydd) Airport.
    Kent 3A **40**
London City Airport. *G Lon* 3C **19**
London Colney. *Herts* 1D **17**
London Gatwick Airport.
    W Sus ....1A **36** & 58
London Heathrow Airport.
    Lon ....1C **25** & 58
London Luton Airport. *Lutn* ....2D **7** & 59
London Southend Airport.
    Essx 3C **21**
London Stansted Airport.
    Essx ....2D **9** & 59
Long Common. *Hants* 1B **42**
Long Crendon. *Buck* 1C **15**
Longcross. *Surr* 2B **24**
Long Ditton. *Surr* 2D **25**
Longfield. *Kent* 2A **28**
Longfield Hill. *Kent* 2A **28**
Longford. *G Lon* 1C **25**
Long Gardens. *Essx* 1C **11**
Long Hanborough. *Oxon* 3A **4**
Longlane. *W Ber* 1A **22**
Long Marston. *Herts* 3A **6**
Longmoor Camp. *Hants* 2D **33**
Longparish. *Hants* 1A **32**
Longstock. *Hants* 2A **32**
Long Sutton. *Hants* 1D **33**
Longwick. *Buck* 1D **15**
Long Wittenham. *Oxon* 2B **14**
Longworth. *Oxon* 2A **14**
Loose. *Kent* 3B **28**
Loosley Row. *Buck* 1A **16**
Lordington. *W Sus* 2D **43**
Loudwater. *Buck* 2B **16**
Loughton. *Essx* 2C **19**
Loughton. *Mil* 1A **6**
Lovedean. *Hants* 1C **43**
Loves Green. *Essx* 1A **20**
Lower Arncott. *Oxon* 3C **5**
Lower Assendon. *Oxon* 3D **15**
Lower Basildon. *W Ber* 1C **23**
Lower Beeding. *W Sus* 3A **36**
Lower Bordean. *Hants* 3C **33**
Lower Bullington. *Hants* 1A **32**
Lower Common. *Hants* 1C **33**
Lower Dicker. *E Sus* 1D **47**
Lower Farringdon. *Hants* 2D **33**
Lower Froyle. *Hants* 1D **33**
Lower Gravenhurst. *C Beds* 1D **7**
Lower Green. *Essx* 1C **9**
Lower Green. *W Ber* 2A **22**
Lower Halstow. *Kent* 2C **29**
Lower Hardres. *Kent* 3B **30**
Lower Heyford. *Oxon* 2A **4**
Lower Higham. *Kent* 1B **28**
Lower Holbrook. *Suff* 1B **12**
Lower Horncroft. *W Sus* 1C **45**
Lower Kingswood. *Surr* 3A **26**
Lower Layham. *Suff* 1A **12**
Lower Nazeing. *Essx* 1B **18**
Lower Rainham. *Medw* 2C **29**
Lower Raydon. *Suff* 1A **12**
Lower Shelton. *C Beds* 1B **6**
Lower Shiplake. *Oxon* 1D **23**
Lower Stoke. *Medw* 1C **29**
Lower Stondon. *C Beds* 1D **7**
Lower Sundon. *C Beds* 2C **7**
Lower Swanwick. *Hants* 2A **42**
Lower Upham. *Hants* 1B **42**
Lower Upnor. *Medw* 1B **28**
Lower Wield. *Hants* 1C **33**
Lower Woodend. *Buck* 3A **16**
Lowfield Heath. *W Sus* 1A **36**
Lowford. *Hants* 2A **42**
Loxhill. *Surr* 2C **35**

Loxwood. *W Sus* 2C **35**
Luddenham. *Kent* 2D **29**
Luddesdown. *Kent* 2A **28**
Ludgershall. *Buck* 3C **5**
Luffenhall. *Herts* 2A **8**
Lullington. *E Sus* 2D **47**
Lunsford. *Kent* 3B **28**
Lunsford's Cross. *E Sus* 1B **48**
Lurgashall. *W Sus* 3B **34**
Luton. *Lutn* 2C **7**
Luton (London) Airport.
    Lutn ....2D **7** & 59
Lydd. *Kent* 3A **40**
Lydden. *Kent* 1C **41**
    (nr. Dover)
Lydden. *Kent* 2D **31**
    (nr. Margate)
Lydd (London Ashford) Airport.
    Kent 3A **40**
Lydd-on-Sea. *Kent* 3A **40**
Lyde Green. *Hants* 3D **23**
Lye Green. *Buck* 1B **16**
Lye Green. *E Sus* 2D **37**
Lyford. *Oxon* 2A **14**
Lymbridge Green. *Kent* 1B **40**
Lyminge. *Kent* 1B **40**
Lyminster. *W Sus* 2C **45**
Lympne. *Kent* 2B **40**
Lyne. *Surr* 2C **25**
Lynsted. *Kent* 2D **29**

M

Mackerye End. *Herts* 3D **7**
Madehurst. *W Sus* 1B **44**
Madingley. *Down* 1A **48**
Magdalen Laver. *Essx* 1D **19**
Magham Down. *E Sus* 1A **48**
Maidenbower. *W Sus* 2A **36**
Maidenhead. *Wind* 3A **16**
Maiden's Green. *Brac* 1A **24**
Maidensgrove. *Oxon* 3D **15**
Maids Moreton. *Buck* 1D **5**
Maidstone. *Kent* 3B **28**
Malden Rushett. *G Lon* 2D **25**
Maldon. *Essx* 1C **21**
Mallows Green. *Essx* 2C **9**
Maltman's Hill. *Kent* 1D **39**
Mannings Heath. *W Sus* 3A **36**
Manningtree. *Essx* 1B **12**
Manor Park. *G Lon* 3C **19**
Manston. *Kent* 2D **31**
Manston Airport. *Kent* 2D **31**
Manuden. *Essx* 2C **9**
Maple Cross. *Herts* 2C **17**
Mapledurham. *Oxon* 1C **23**
Mapledurwell. *Hants* 3C **23**
Maplehurst. *W Sus* 3D **35**
Maplescombe. *Kent* 2D **27**
Marcham. *Oxon* 2A **14**
Marchwood. *Hants* 1A **42**
Marden. *Kent* 1B **38**
Marden Beech. *Kent* 1B **38**
Marden Thorn. *Kent* 1B **38**
Marehill. *W Sus* 1C **45**
Maresfield. *E Sus* 3C **37**
Margaret Roding. *Essx* 3D **9**
Margaretting. *Essx* 1A **20**
Margaretting Tye. *Essx* 1A **20**
Margate. *Kent* 1D **31**
Margery. *Surr* 3A **26**
Marine Town. *Kent* 1D **29**
Markbeech. *Kent* 1C **37**
Mark Cross. *E Sus* 2D **37**
Mark's Corner. *IOW* 3A **42**
Marks Tey. *Essx* 2D **11**
Markyate. *Herts* 3C **7**
Marle Green. *E Sus* 1D **47**
Marlow. *Buck* 3A **16**
Marlow Bottom. *Buck* 3A **16**
Marlow Common. *Buck* 3A **16**
Marlpit Hill. *Kent* 1C **37**
Marlpits. *E Sus* 3C **37**
Marsh. *Buck* 1A **16**
Marshalswick. *Herts* 1D **17**
Marsh Baldon. *Oxon* 2B **14**
Marsh Benham. *W Ber* 2A **22**
Marshborough. *Kent* 3D **31**
Marshbury. *Essx* 3A **10**
Marsh Gibbon. *Buck* 2C **5**
Marsh Green. *Kent* 1C **37**
Marshside. *Kent* 2C **31**
Marston. *Oxon* 1B **14**
Marston Moretaine. *C Beds* 1B **6**
Marston St Lawrence. *Nptn* 1B **4**
Marsworth. *Herts* 3B **6**
Martin. *Kent* 1D **41**
Martin Mill. *Kent* 1D **41**
Martyr's Green. *Surr* 3C **25**
Martyr Worthy. *Hants* 2B **32**
Marylebone. *G Lon* 3A **18**
Mashbury. *Essx* 3A **10**
Matching. *Essx* 3D **9**
Matching Green. *Essx* 3D **9**
Matching Tye. *Essx* 3D **9**
Matfield. *Kent* 1A **38**
Mattingley. *Hants* 3D **23**

Maulden. *C Beds* 1C **7**
Maxted Street. *Kent* 1B **40**
Maxton. *Kent* 1C **41**
Maybush. *Sotn* 1A **42**
Mayes Green. *Surr* 2D **35**
Mayfield. *E Sus* 3D **37**
Mayford. *Surr* 3B **24**
Maylandsea. *Essx* 1D **21**
Maylandsea. *Essx* 1D **21**
Maynard's Green. *E Sus* 1D **47**
Maypole. *Kent* 2C **31**
Meadle. *Buck* 1A **16**
Meath Green. *Surr* 1A **36**
Medmenham. *Buck* 3A **16**
Medstead. *Hants* 2C **33**
Medway Towns. *Medw* ....2B **28** & 54
Meesden. *Herts* 1C **9**
Mentmore. *Buck* 3B **6**
Meon. *Hants* 2B **42**
Meonstoke. *Hants* 3C **33**
Meopham. *Kent* 2A **28**
Meopham Green. *Kent* 2A **28**
Meopham Station. *Kent* 2A **28**
Meppershall. *C Beds* 1D **7**
Mereworth. *Kent* 3A **28**
Merrow. *Surr* 3C **25**
Mersham. *Kent* 2A **40**
Merstham. *Surr* 3A **26**
Merston. *W Sus* 2A **44**
Merton. *G Lon* 2A **26**
Merton. *Oxon* 3B **4**
Messing. *Essx* 3C **11**
Micheldever. *Hants* 2B **32**
Micheldever Station. *Hants* 1B **32**
Michelmersh. *Hants* 3A **32**
Micklefield Green. *Herts* 2C **17**
Mickleham. *Surr* 3D **25**
Middle Assendon. *Oxon* 3D **15**
Middle Aston. *Oxon* 2A **4**
Middle Barton. *Oxon* 2A **4**
Middle Claydon. *Buck* 2D **5**
Middleton. *Essx* 1C **11**
Middleton. *Hants* 1A **32**
Middleton Cheney. *Nptn* 1B **4**
Middleton-on-Sea. *W Sus* 3B **44**
Middleton Stoney. *Oxon* 2B **4**
Midgham. *W Ber* 2B **22**
Midhurst. *W Sus* 3A **34**
Mid Lavant. *W Sus* 2A **44**
Milcombe. *Oxon* 1A **4**
Milebush. *Kent* 1B **38**
Mile End. *Essx* 2D **11**
Mile Oak. *Brig* 2A **46**
Mile Town. *Kent* 1D **29**
Milford. *Surr* 1B **34**
Milland. *W Sus* 2D **33**
Millbridge. *Surr* 1A **34**
Millbrook. *C Beds* 1C **7**
Millbrook. *Sotn* 1A **42**
Mill Corner. *E Sus* 3C **39**
Mill End. *Buck* 3D **15**
Mill End. *Herts* 1B **8**
Mill Green. *Essx* 1A **20**
Mill Green. *Suff* 1D **11**
Mill Hill. *G Lon* 2A **18**
Mill Lane. *Hants* 3D **23**
Millow. *C Beds* 1A **8**
Milstead. *Kent* 3D **29**
Milton. *Cumb* 1A **4**
Milton. *Oxon* 2A **14**
Milton. *Port* 3C **43**
Milton Bryan. *C Beds* 1B **6**
Milton Common. *Oxon* 1C **15**
Milton Hill. *Oxon* 2A **14**
Milton Keynes. *Mil* ....1A **6** & 55
Milton Keynes Village. *Mil* 1A **6**
Milton Regis. *Kent* 2C **29**
Milton Street. *E Sus* 2D **47**
Mimbridge. *Surr* 2B **24**
Minsted. *W Sus* 3A **34**
Minster. *Kent* 2D **31**
    (nr. Ramsgate)
Minster. *Kent* 1D **29**
    (nr. Sheerness)
Mistley. *Essx* 1B **12**
Mistley Heath. *Essx* 1B **12**
Mitcham. *G Lon* 2A **26**
Mixbury. *Oxon* 1C **5**
Molash. *Kent* 3A **30**
Molehill Green. *Essx* 2D **9**
Moneyrow Green. *Wind* 1A **24**
Monken Hadley. *G Lon* 2A **18**
Monk's Gate. *W Sus* 3A **36**
Monk Sherborne. *Hants* 3C **23**
Monks Risborough. *Buck* 1A **16**
Monk Street. *Essx* 2A **10**
Monkton. *Kent* 2C **31**
Monkwood. *Hants* 2C **33**
Moon's Green. *Kent* 3C **39**
Moorgreen. *Hants* 1A **42**
Moorhouse. *Surr* 3C **27**
Moor, The. *Kent* 3B **38**
Morden. *G Lon* 2A **26**
Morestead. *Hants* 3B **32**
Moreton. *Essx* 1D **19**
Moreton. *Oxon* 1C **15**
Morris Green. *Essx* 1B **10**

Mortimer. *W Ber* 2C **23**
Mortimer West End. *Hants* 2C **23**
Mottingham. *G Lon* 1C **27**
Mott's Mill. *E Sus* 2D **37**
Moulsecoomb. *Brig* 2B **46**
Moulsford. *Oxon* 3B **14**
Moulsoe. *Mil* 1B **6**
Mountain Street. *Kent* 3A **30**
Mount Bures. *Essx* 1D **11**
Mountfield. *E Sus* 3B **38**
Mountnessing. *Essx* 2A **20**
Mount Pleasant. *Buck* 1C **5**
Mount Pleasant. *E Sus* 1C **47**
Mount Skippett. *Oxon* 3A **4**
Much Hadham. *Herts* 3C **9**
Mucking. *Thur* 3A **20**
Mugswell. *Surr* 3A **26**
Mundon. *Essx* 1C **21**
Murcott. *Oxon* 3B **4**
Murrell Green. *Hants* 3D **23**
Mursley. *Buck* 2A **6**
Muswell Hill. *G Lon* 3A **18**
Mytchett. *Surr* 3A **24**

N

Nackington. *Kent* 3B **30**
Nacton. *Suff* 1C **13**
Nalderswood. *Surr* 1A **36**
Naphill. *Buck* 2A **16**
Nash. *Buck* 1D **5**
Nash. *Kent* 3C **31**
Nash Lee. *Buck* 1A **16**
Nasty. *Herts* 2B **8**
Nately Scures. *Hants* 3D **23**
Navestock Heath.
   Essx 2D **19**
Navestock Side. *Essx* 2D **19**
Nayland. *Suff* 1D **11**
Nazeing. *Essx* 1C **19**
Neasden. *G Lon* 3A **18**
Neithrop. *Oxon* 1A **4**
Nethercott. *Oxon* 2A **4**
Netherfield. *E Sus* 1B **48**
Nether Street. *Essx* 3D **9**
Netherton. *Hants* 3A **22**
Nether Winchendon.
   Buck 3D **5**
Nether Worton. *Oxon* 1A **4**
Netley. *Hants* 2A **42**
Nettlebed. *Oxon* 3D **15**
Nettleden. *Herts* 3C **7**
Nettlestead. *Kent* 3A **28**
Nettlestead Green. *Kent* 3A **28**
Nettlestone. *IOW* 3C **43**
Nevendon. *Essx* 2B **20**
New Addington. *G Lon* 2B **26**
New Alresford. *Hants* 2B **32**
New Ash Green. *Kent* 2A **28**
New Barn. *Kent* 2A **28**
Newbottle. *Nptn* 1B **4**
Newbourne. *Suff* 1C **13**
Newbridge. *IOW* 3A **42**
New Brighton. *Hants* 2D **43**
Newbury. *W Ber* 2A **22**
Newchapel. *Surr* 1B **36**
New Cheriton. *Hants* 3B **32**
Newchurch. *Kent* 2A **40**
New Denham. *Buck* 3C **17**
Newdigate. *Surr* 1D **35**
Newell Green. *Brac* 1A **24**
New Eltham. *G Lon* 1C **27**
Newenden. *Kent* 3C **39**
New England. *Essx* 1B **10**
Newfound. *Hants* 3B **22**
Newgate Street. *Herts* 1B **18**
New Greens. *Herts* 1D **17**
Newhaven. *E Sus* . . . . . . .2C **47** & **60**
New Haw. *Surr* 2C **25**
New Hythe. *Kent* 3B **28**
Newick. *E Sus* 3C **37**
Newingreen. *Kent* 2B **40**
Newington. *Kent* 2B **40**
   (nr. Folkestone)
Newington. *Kent* 2C **29**
   (nr. Sittingbourne)
Newington. *Oxon* 2C **15**
Newlands. *Essx* 3C **21**
New Malden. *G Lon* 2A **26**
Newman's Green. *Suff* 1C **11**
New Mill. *Herts* 3B **6**
New Mistley. *Essx* 1B **12**
Newnham. *Hants* 3D **23**
Newnham. *Herts* 1A **8**
Newnham. *Kent* 3D **29**
Newport. *Essx* 1D **9**
Newport. *IOW* 3B **42**
Newport Pagnell. *Mil* 1A **6**
Newpound Common.
   W Sus .3C **35**
New Romney. *Kent* 3A **40**
Newton. *Suff* 1D **11**
Newton Longville. *Buck* 1A **6**
Newton Purcell. *Oxon* 1C **5**
Newton Stacey. *Hants* 1A **32**
Newton Valence. *Hants* 2D **33**

Newtown. *Hants* 1B **42**
   (nr. Bishop's Waltham)
Newtown. *Hants* 2A **34**
   (nr. Liphook)
Newtown. *Hants* 2A **22**
   (nr. Newbury)
Newtown. *Hants* 2A **42**
   (nr. Warsash)
Newtown. *Hants* 1C **43**
   (nr. Wickham)
Newtown. *IOW* 3A **42**
New Town. *Lutn* 2C **7**
New Yatt. *Oxon* 3A **4**
Newyears Green. *G Lon* 3C **17**
Nine Ashes. *Essx* 1D **19**
Ninfield. *E Sus* 1B **48**
Ningwood. *IOW* 3A **42**
Noak Hill. *G Lon* 2D **19**
Noke. *Oxon* 3B **4**
Nonington. *Kent* 3C **31**
Norleywood. *Hants* 3A **42**
Normandy. *Surr* 3B **24**
Norman's Bay. *E Sus* 2A **48**
Northall. *Buck* 2B **6**
Northam. *Sotn* 1A **42**
North Ascot. *Brac* 2B **24**
North Aston. *Oxon* 2A **4**
Northaw. *Herts* 1A **18**
North Baddesley. *Hants* 3A **32**
North Benfleet. *Essx* 3B **20**
North Bersted. *W Sus* 2B **44**
North Boarhunt. *Hants* 1C **43**
Northbourne. *Kent* 3D **31**
Northbourne. *Oxon* 3B **14**
Northbrook. *Oxon* 2A **4**
North Chailey. *E Sus* 3B **36**
Northchapel. *W Sus* 3B **34**
Northchurch. *Herts* 1B **16**
North Common. *E Sus* 3B **36**
Northcourt. *Oxon* 2B **14**
North Cray. *G Lon* 1C **27**
Northend. *Buck* 2D **15**
North End. *Essx* 3A **10**
   (nr. Great Dunmow)
North End. *Essx* 1B **10**
   (nr. Great Yeldham)
North End. *Hants* 2A **22**
North End. *Port* 2C **43**
North End. *W Sus* 2C **45**
North Fambridge. *Essx* 2C **21**
Northfleet. *Kent* 1A **28**
North Halling. *Medw* 2B **28**
North Hayling. *Hants* 2D **43**
North Heath. *W Sus* 3C **35**
North Hinksey Village. *Oxon* 1A **14**
North Holmwood. *Surr* 1D **35**
Northiam. *E Sus* 3C **39**
Northington. *Hants* 2B **32**
North Lancing. *W Sus* 2D **45**
North Lee. *Buck* 1A **16**
North Leigh. *Kent* 1B **40**
North Leigh. *Oxon* 3A **4**
North Marden. *W Sus* 1A **44**
North Marston. *Buck* 2D **5**
Northmoor. *Oxon* 1A **14**
North Moreton. *Oxon* 3B **14**
North Mundham. *W Sus* 2A **44**
North Newington. *Oxon* 1A **4**
Northney. *Hants* 2D **43**
North Oakley. *Hants* 3B **22**
North Ockendon. *G Lon* 3D **19**
Northolt. *G Lon* 3D **17**
North Sheen. *G Lon* 1D **25**
North Shoebury. *S'end* 3D **21**
North Stifford. *Thur* 3A **20**
North Stoke. *Oxon* 3C **15**
North Stoke. *W Sus* 1C **45**
North Street. *Hants* 2C **33**
North Street. *Kent* 3A **30**
North Street. *Medw* 1C **29**
North Street. *W Ber* 1C **23**
North Waltham. *Hants* 1B **32**
North Warnborough. *Hants* 3D **23**
North Weald Bassett. *Essx* 1D **19**
North Weston. *Oxon* 1C **15**
Northwood. *G Lon* 2C **17**
Northwood. *IOW* 3A **42**
Northwood. *Kent* 2D **31**
Norton. *Herts* 1A **8**
Norton. *W Sus* 2B **44**
   (nr. Arundel)
Norton. *W Sus* 3A **44**
   (nr. Selsey)
Norton Green. *IOW* 3A **42**
Norton Heath. *Essx* 1A **20**
Norton Mandeville. *Essx* 1D **19**
Norwood Hill. *Surr* 1A **36**
Nounsley. *Essx* 3B **10**
Nuffield. *Oxon* 3C **15**
Nuneham Courtenay. *Oxon* 2B **14**
Nursling. *Hants* 1A **42**
Nursted. *W Sus* 3D **33**
Nutbourne. *W Sus* 2D **43**
   (nr. Chichester)
Nutbourne. *W Sus* 1C **45**
   (nr. Pulborough)
Nutfield. *Surr* 3B **26**

Nuthampstead. *Herts* 1C **9**
Nuthurst. *W Sus* 3D **35**
Nutley. *E Sus* 3C **37**
Nyetimber. *W Sus* 3A **44**
Nyewood. *W Sus* 3A **34**
Nyton. *W Sus* 2B **44**

O

Oad Street. *Kent* 2C **29**
Oakhanger. *Hants* 2D **33**
Oakley. *Buck* 3C **5**
Oakley. *Hants* 3B **22**
Oakley Green. *Wind* 1B **24**
Oakshott. *Hants* 3D **33**
Oakwoodhill. *Surr* 2D **35**
Oare. *Kent* .2A **30**
Oare. *W Ber* 1B **22**
Ockham. *Surr* 3C **25**
Ockley. *Surr* 1D **35**
Oddington. *Oxon* 3B **4**
Odiham. *Hants* 3D **23**
Odsey. *Cambs* 1A **8**
Offham. *E Sus* 1C **47**
Offham. *Kent* 3A **28**
Offham. *W Sus* 2C **45**
Offley Hoo. *Herts* 2D **7**
Old Alresford. *Hants* 2B **32**
Old Basing. *Hants* 3C **23**
Old Bexley. *G Lon* 1C **27**
Old Burghclere. *Hants* 3A **22**
Old Coulsdon. *G Lon* 3B **26**
Old Felixstowe. *Suff* 1D **13**
Old Heathfield. *E Sus* 3D **37**
Old Knebworth. *Herts* 2A **8**
Old Romney. *Kent* 3A **40**
Old Stratford. *Nptn* 1D **5**
Old Town. *E Sus* 3D **47**
Old Warden. *C Beds* 1D **7**
Old Windsor. *Wind* 1B **24**
Old Wives Lees. *Kent* 3A **30**
Old Woking. *Surr* 3C **25**
Old Woodstock. *Oxon* 3A **4**
Oliver's Battery. *Hants* 3A **32**
Olmstead Green. *Cambs* 1A **10**
Onslow Green. *Essx* 3A **10**
Onslow Village. *Surr* 1B **34**
Ore. *E Sus* .1C **49**
Oreham Common. *W Sus* 1A **46**
Orlestone. *Kent* 2D **39**
Orpington. *G Lon* 2C **27**
Orsett. *Thur* 3A **20**
Ospringe. *Kent* 2A **30**
Ostend. *Essx* 2D **21**
Osterley. *G Lon* 1D **25**
Otford. *Kent* 3D **27**
Otham. *Kent* 3B **28**
Otterbourne. *Hants* 3A **32**
Otterham Quay. *Kent* 2C **29**
Ottershaw. *Surr* 2C **25**
Otterwood. *Hants* 2A **42**
Ottinge. *Kent* 1B **40**
Outwood. *Surr* 1B **36**
Over Kiddington. *Oxon* 2A **4**
Oversland. *Kent* 3A **30**
Overthorpe. *Nptn* 1A **4**
Overton. *Hants* 1B **32**
Over Worton. *Oxon* 2A **4**
Oving. *Buck* 2D **5**
Oving. *W Sus* 2B **44**
Ovingdean. *Brig* 2B **46**
Ovington. *Essx* 1B **10**
Ovington. *Hants* 2B **32**
Ower. *Hants* 2A **42**
Owlsmoor. *Brac* 2A **24**
Owlswick. *Buck* 1D **15**
Ownham. *W Ber* 1A **22**
Owslebury. *Hants* 3B **32**
Oxen End. *Essx* 2A **10**
Oxford. *Oxon* . . . . .1B **14** & **55**
Oxhey. *Herts* 2D **17**
Oxley Green. *Essx* 3D **11**
Oxley's Green. *E Sus* 3A **38**
Oxshott. *Surr* 2D **25**
Oxted. *Surr* 3B **26**

P

Pachesham. *Surr* 3D **25**
Padbury. *Buck* 1D **5**
Paddington. *G Lon* 3A **18**
Paddlesworth. *Kent* 2B **40**
Paddock. *Kent* 3D **29**
Paddock Wood. *Kent* 1A **38**
Padworth. *W Ber* 2C **23**
Pagham. *W Sus* 3A **44**
Paglesham Churchend. *Essx* 2D **21**
Paglesham Eastend. *Essx* 2D **21**
Paine's Corner. *E Sus* 3A **38**
Painter's Forstal. *Kent* 3D **29**
Palehouse Common. *E Sus* 1C **47**
Paley Street. *Wind* 1A **24**
Palmarsh. *Kent* 2B **40**
Pamber End. *Hants* 3C **23**
Pamber Green. *Hants* 3C **23**

Pamber Heath. *Hants* 2C **23**
Panfield. *Essx* 2B **10**
Pangbourne. *W Ber* 1C **23**
Paramour Street. *Kent* 2C **31**
Parbrook. *W Sus* 3C **35**
Pardown. *Hants* 1B **32**
Park Corner. *E Sus* 2D **37**
Park Corner. *Oxon* 3C **15**
Parkeston. *Essx* 1C **13**
Park Gate. *Hants* 2B **42**
Parkgate. *Surr* 1A **36**
Parkhurst. *IOW* 3A **42**
Park Street. *Herts* 1D **17**
Park Street. *W Sus* 2D **35**
Park Town. *Oxon* 1B **14**
Parmoor. *Buck* 3D **15**
Parsonage Green. *Essx* 3B **10**
Partridge Green. *W Sus* 1D **45**
Passenham. *Nptn* 1D **5**
Passfield. *Hants* 2A **34**
Passingford Bridge. *Essx* 2D **19**
Patcham. *Brig* 2B **46**
Patchetts Green. *Herts* 2D **17**
Patching. *W Sus* 2C **45**
Patmore Heath. *Herts* 2C **9**
Patrixbourne. *Kent* 3B **30**
Pattiswick. *Essx* 2C **11**
Peacehaven. *E Sus* 2C **47**
Peasemore. *W Ber* 1A **22**
Pease Pottage. *W Sus* 2A **36**
Peaslake. *Surr* 1C **35**
Peasmarsh. *E Sus* 3C **39**
Peasmarsh. *Surr* 1B **34**
Pebmarsh. *Essx* 1C **11**
Peckham Bush. *Kent* 3A **28**
Pedlinge. *Kent* 2B **40**
Peel Common. *Hants* 2B **42**
Peening Quarter. *Kent* 3C **39**
Pegsdon. *C Beds* 1D **7**
Peldon. *Essx* 3D **11**
Pembury. *Kent* 1A **38**
Penge. *G Lon* 1B **26**
Penhurst. *E Sus* 1A **48**
Penn. *Buck* .2B **16**
Penn Street. *Buck* 2B **16**
Penshurst. *Kent* 1D **37**
Peper Harow. *Surr* 1B **34**
Perry Green. *Essx* 2C **11**
Perry Green. *Herts* 3C **9**
Perry Street. *Kent* 1A **28**
Perrywood. *Kent* 3A **30**
Petersfield. *Hants* 3D **33**
Peter's Green. *Herts* 3D **7**
Petham. *Kent* 3B **30**
Pett. *E Sus* .1C **49**
Pett Bottom. *Kent* 3B **30**
Petteridge. *Kent* 1A **38**
Petts Wood. *G Lon* 2C **27**
Petworth. *W Sus* 3B **34**
Pevensey. *E Sus* 2A **48**
Pevensey Bay. *E Sus* 2A **48**
Pheasants Hill. *Buck* 3D **15**
Phoenix Green. *Hants* 3D **23**
Piccotts End. *Herts* 1C **17**
Picket Piece. *Hants* 1A **32**
Piddinghoe. *E Sus* 2C **47**
Piddington. *Buck* 2A **16**
Piddington. *Oxon* 3C **5**
Pilgrims Hatch. *Essx* 2D **19**
Piltdown. *E Sus* 3C **37**
Pinkneys Green. *Wind* 3A **16**
Pinmill. *Suff* .1C **13**
Pinner. *G Lon* 3D **17**
Pirbright. *Surr* 3B **24**
Pirton. *Herts* 1D **7**
Pishill. *Oxon* 3D **15**
Pitch Green. *Buck* 1D **15**
Pitch Place. *Surr* 3B **24**
Pitsea. *Essx* 3B **20**
Pitstone. *Buck* 3B **6**
Pitt. *Hants* 3A **32**
Pittswood. *Kent* 1A **38**
Plaistow. *W Sus* 2C **35**
Plastow Green. *Hants* 2B **22**
Platt. *Kent* 3A **28**
Platt's Heath. *Kent* 3C **29**
Platt, The. *E Sus* 2D **37**
Plaxtol. *Kent* 3A **28**
Playden. *E Sus* 3D **39**
Play Hatch. *Oxon* 1D **23**
Pledgdon Green. *Essx* 2D **9**
Pleshey. *Essx* 3A **10**
Pluckley. *Kent* 1D **39**
Plucks Gutter. *Kent* 2C **31**
Plummers Plain. *W Sus* 3A **36**
Plumpton. *E Sus* 1B **46**
Plumpton Green. *E Sus* 1B **46**
Plumstead. *G Lon* 1C **27**
Poffley End. *Oxon* 3A **4**
Point Clear. *Essx* 3A **12**
Polegate. *E Sus* 2D **47**
Poling. *W Sus* 2C **45**
Poling Corner. *W Sus* 2C **45**
Pollicott. *Buck* 3D **5**
Polstead. *Suff* 1D **11**
Polstead Heath. *Suff* 1D **11**

Ponders End. *G Lon* 2B **18**
Pond Street. *Essx* 1C **9**
Pondtail. *Hants* 3A **24**
Ponts Green. *E Sus* 1A **48**
Pooksgreen. *Hants* 1A **42**
Pool Street. *Essx* 1B **10**
Pootings. *Kent* 1C **37**
Popeswood. *Brac* 2A **24**
Popham. *Hants* 1B **32**
Poplar. *G Lon* 3B **18**
Popley. *Hants* 3C **23**
Porchfield. *IOW* 3A **42**
Portchester. *Hants* 2C **43**
Portsea. *Port* 2C **43**
Portslade-by-Sea. *Brig* 2A **46**
Portsmouth. *Port* . . . . . . .3C **43, 56 & 60**
Port Solent. *Port* 2C **43**
Portswood. *Sotn* 1A **42**
Postcombe. *Oxon* 2D **15**
Postling. *Kent* 2B **40**
Potsgrove. *C Beds* 2B **6**
Potten End. *Herts* 1C **17**
Potters Bar. *Herts* 1A **18**
Potters Crouch. *Herts* 1D **17**
Potterspury. *Nptn* 1D **5**
Potter Street. *Essx* 1C **19**
Poundfield. *E Sus* 2D **37**
Poundgate. *E Sus* 3C **37**
Pound Green. *E Sus* 3D **37**
Pound Hill. *W Sus* 2A **36**
Poundon. *Buck* 2C **5**
Pound Street. *Hants* 2A **22**
Pounsley. *E Sus* 3D **37**
Poyle. *Slo* 1C **25**
Poynings. *W Sus* 1A **46**
Pratt's Bottom. *G Lon* 2C **27**
Preston. *Brig* 2B **46**
Preston. *Herts* 2D **7**
Preston. *Kent* 2C **31**
. . . .(nr. Canterbury)
Preston. *Kent* 2A **30**
. . . .(nr. Faversham)
Preston Bissett. *Buck* 2C **5**
Preston Candover. *Hants* 1C **33**
Prestwood. *Buck* 1A **16**
Priestwood. *Brac* 1A **24**
Priestwood. *Kent* 2A **28**
Princes Risborough. *Buck* 1A **16**
Prinsted. *W Sus* 2D **43**
Prittlewell. *S'end* 3C **21**
Privett. *Hants* 3C **33**
Puckeridge. *Herts* 2B **8**
Pulborough. *W Sus* 1C **45**
Pulloxhill. *C Beds* 1C **7**
Punnett's Town. *E Sus* 3A **38**
Purbrook. *Hants* 2C **43**
Purfleet. *Thur* 1D **27**
Purleigh. *Essx* 1C **21**
Purley. *G Lon* 2B **26**
Purley on Thames. *W Ber* 1C **23**
Pusey. *Oxon* 2A **14**
Putney. *G Lon* 1A **26**
Puttenham. *Herts* 3A **6**
Puttenham. *Surr* 1B **34**
Puttock End. *Essx* 1C **11**
Puttock's End. *Essx* 3D **9**
Pyecombe. *W Sus* 1A **46**
Pye Corner. *Herts* 3C **9**
Pyrford. *Surr* 3C **25**
Pyrford Village. *Surr* 3C **25**
Pyrton. *Oxon* 2C **15**

Q

Quainton. *Buck* 2D **5**
Quarrendon. *Buck* 3A **6**
Queenborough. *Kent* 1D **29**
Queen Street. *Kent* 1A **38**
Quendon. *Essx* 1D **9**
Quick's Green. *W Ber* 1B **22**
Quidhampton. *Hants* 3B **22**

R

Rableyheath. *Herts* 3A **8**
Rack End. *Oxon* 1A **14**
Rackham. *W Sus* 1C **45**
Radclive. *Buck* 1C **5**
Radfall. *Kent* 2B **30**
Radford. *Oxon* 2A **4**
Radlett. *Herts* 2D **17**
Radley. *Oxon* 2B **14**
Radnage. *Buck* 2D **15**
Radstone. *Nptn* 1B **4**
Radwell. *Herts* 1A **8**
Radwinter. *Essx* 1A **10**
Rainham. *G Lon* 3D **19**
Rainham. *Medw* 2C **29**
Rake. *W Sus* 3A **34**
Ram Lane. *Kent* 1D **39**
Ramsdean. *Hants* 3D **33**
Ramsdell. *Hants* 3B **22**
Ramsden. *Oxon* 3A **4**
Ramsden Bellhouse. *Essx* 2B **20**
Ramsden Heath. *Essx* 2B **20**

Ramsey. *Essx* 1C **13**
Ramsey Island. *Essx* 1D **21**
Ramsgate. *Kent* 2D **31**
Ramsnest Common. *Surr* 2B **34**
Rank's Green. *Essx* 3B **10**
Ranmore Common. *Surr* 3D **25**
Ratton Village. *E Sus* 2D **47**
Rawreth. *Essx* 2B **20**
Raydon. *Suff* 1A **12**
Rayleigh. *Essx* 2C **21**
Rayne. *Essx* .2B **10**
Rayners Lane. *G Lon* 3D **17**
Reading. *Read* . . . . .1D **23 & 56**
Reading Street. *Kent* 2D **39**
Reculver. *Kent* 2C **31**
Redbourn. *Herts* 3D **7**
Redford. *W Sus* 3A **34**
Redhill. *Surr* 3A **26**
Reed. *Herts* 1B **8**
Reed End. *Herts* 1B **8**
Reigate. *Surr* 3A **26**
Remenham. *Wok* 3D **15**
Remenham Hill. *Wok* 3D **15**
Rettendon. *Essx* 2B **20**
Rew Street. *IOW* 3A **42**
Rhodes Minnis. *Kent* 1B **40**
Richborough Port. *Kent* 2D **31**
Richings Park. *Buck* 1C **25**
Richmond. *G Lon* 1D **25**
Rickling. *Essx* 1C **9**
Rickling Green. *Essx* 2D **9**
Rickmansworth. *Herts* 2C **17**
Ridge. *Herts* 1A **18**
Ridgewell. *Essx* 1B **10**
Ridgewood. *E Sus* 3C **37**
Ridgmont. *C Beds* 1B **6**
Ridley. *Kent* .2A **28**
Ringlestone. *Kent* 3C **29**
Ringmer. *E Sus* 1C **47**
Ringshall. *Buck* 3B **6**
Ringwould. *Kent* 1D **41**
Ripe. *E Sus* .1D **47**
Ripley. *Surr* .3C **25**
Riplington. *Hants* 3C **33**
Ripple. *Kent* 1D **41**
Riseden. *E Sus* 2A **38**
Riseden. *Kent* 2B **38**
Riseley. *Wok* 2D **23**
Rivenhall. *Essx* 3C **11**
Rivenhall End. *Essx* 3C **11**
River. *Kent* .1C **41**
River. *W Sus* 3B **34**
Riverhead. *Kent* 3D **27**
Robertsbridge. *E Sus* 3B **38**
Robinhood End. *Essx* 1B **10**
Rochester. *Medw* . . .2B **28 & Medway 54**
Rochford. *Essx* 2C **21**
Rock. *W Sus* 1D **45**
Rockwell End. *Buck* 3D **15**
Rodmell. *E Sus* 2C **47**
Rodmersham. *Kent* 2D **29**
Rodmersham Green. *Kent* 2D **29**
Roe Green. *Herts* 1B **8**
Roehampton. *G Lon* 1A **26**
Roffey. *W Sus* 2D **35**
Rogate. *W Sus* 3A **34**
Roke. *Oxon* .2C **15**
Rokemarsh. *Oxon* 2C **15**
Rolvenden. *Kent* 2C **39**
Rolvenden Layne. *Kent* 2C **39**
Romford. *G Lon* 3D **19**
Romsey. *Hants* 3A **32**
Rookwood. *W Sus* 3D **43**
Ropley. *Hants* 2C **33**
Ropley Dean. *Hants* 2C **33**
Rose Green. *Essx* 2D **11**
Rose Hill. *E Sus* 1C **47**
Roser's Cross. *E Sus* 3D **37**
Rotherfield. *E Sus* 3D **37**
Rotherfield Greys. *Oxon* 3D **15**
Rotherfield Peppard. *Oxon* 3D **15**
Rotherwick. *Hants* 3D **23**
Rotten Row. *W Ber* 1B **22**
Rottingdean. *Brig* 2B **46**
Rough Common. *Kent* 3B **30**
Roundbush Green. *Essx* 3D **9**
Roundhurst. *W Sus* 2B **34**
Round Maple. *Suff* 1D **11**
Roundstreet Common. *W Sus* 3C **35**
Rousham. *Oxon* 2A **4**
Rout's Green. *Buck* 2D **15**
Row Ash. *Hants* 1B **42**
Row Green. *Essx* 2B **10**
Row Heath. *Essx* 3B **12**
Rowhedge. *Essx* 2A **12**
Rowhook. *W Sus* 2D **35**
Rowland's Castle. *Hants* 1D **43**
Rowledge. *Surr* 1A **34**
Rowly. *Surr* .1C **35**
Rowner. *Hants* 2B **42**
Rownhams. *Hants* 1A **42**
Rowsham. *Buck* 3A **6**
Rowstock. *Oxon* 3A **14**
Row Town. *Surr* 2C **25**
Roxwell. *Essx* 1A **20**
Royal Tunbridge Wells. *Kent* 2D **37**

Roydon. *Essx* .3C **9**
Roydon Hamlet. *Essx* 1C **19**
Royston. *Herts* 1B **8**
Ruckinge. *Kent* 2A **40**
Rucklers Lane. *Herts* 1C **17**
Rudgwick. *W Sus* 2C **35**
Rudley Green. *Essx* 1C **21**
Ruislip. *G Lon* 3C **17**
Ruislip Common. *G Lon* 3C **17**
Runcton. *W Sus* 2A **44**
Runfold. *Surr* 1A **34**
Runwell. *Essx* 2B **20**
Ruscombe. *Wok* 1D **23**
Rushden. *Herts* 1B **8**
Rushenden. *Kent* 1D **29**
Rush Green. *Herts* 2A **8**
Rushlake Green. *E Sus* 1A **48**
Rushmoor. *Surr* 1A **34**
Rusper. *W Sus* 2A **36**
Russell's Water. *Oxon* 3D **15**
Russ Hill. *Surr* 1A **36**
Rusthall. *Kent* 2D **37**
Rustington. *W Sus* 2C **45**
Ryarsh. *Kent* 3A **28**
Ryde. *IOW* .3B **42**
Rye. *E Sus* 3D **39**
Rye Foreign. *E Sus* 3D **39**
Rye Harbour. *E Sus* 1D **49**

S

Sacombe. *Herts* 3B **8**
Saddlescombe. *W Sus* 1A **46**
Saffron Walden. *Essx* 1D **9**
St Albans. *Herts* 1D **17**
St Cross. *Hants* 3A **32**
St George's Hill. *Surr* 2C **25**
St Giles's Hill. *Hants* 3A **32**
St Helens. *E Sus* 1C **49**
St Helens. *IOW* 3C **43**
Saint Hill. *W Sus* 2B **36**
St Ippolyts. *Herts* 2D **7**
St Lawrence. *Essx* 1D **21**
St Leonards. *Buck* 1B **16**
St Leonards. *E Sus* 2B **48**
St Margaret's. *Herts* 3C **9**
. . . .(nr. Hemel Hempstead)
St Margarets. *Herts* 1D **19**
. . . .(nr. Hoddesdon)
St Margaret's at Cliffe. *Kent* 1D **41**
St Mary Bourne. *Hants* 3A **22**
St Mary Cray. *G Lon* 2C **27**
St Mary Hoo. *Medw* 1C **29**
St Mary in the Marsh. *Kent* 3A **40**
St Mary's Bay. *Kent* 3A **40**
St Michaels. *Kent* 2C **39**
St Nicholas at Wade. *Kent* 2C **31**
St Osyth. *Essx* 3B **12**
St Osyth Heath. *Essx* 3B **12**
St Paul's Cray. *G Lon* 2C **27**
St Paul's Walden. *Herts* 2D **7**
St Peter's. *Kent* 2D **31**
Salcott. *Essx* 3D **11**
Salehurst. *E Sus* 3B **38**
Salford. *C Beds* 1B **6**
Salfords. *Surr* 1A **36**
Saltdean. *Brig* 2B **46**
Saltwood. *Kent* 2B **40**
Sanderstead. *G Lon* 2B **26**
Sandford-on-Thames. *Oxon* 1B **14**
Sandford St Martin. *Oxon* 2A **4**
Sandgate. *Kent* 2B **40**
Sandhills. *Oxon* 1B **14**
Sandhills. *Surr* 2B **34**
Sandhurst. *Brac* 2A **24**
Sandhurst. *Kent* 3B **38**
Sandhurst Cross. *Kent* 3B **38**
Sandling. *Kent* 3B **28**
Sandon. *Essx* 1B **20**
Sandon. *Herts* 1B **8**
Sandridge. *Herts* 3D **7**
Sands, The. *Surr* 1A **34**
Sandway. *Kent* 3C **29**
Sandwich. *Kent* 3D **31**
Sandy. *C Beds* 1A **8**
Sarisbury. *Hants* 2B **42**
Sarratt. *Herts* 2C **17**
Sarre. *Kent* .2C **31**
Satwell. *Oxon* 3D **15**
Saunderton. *Buck* 1D **15**
Saunderton Lee. *Buck* 2A **16**
Sawbridgeworth. *Herts* 3C **9**
Sayers Common. *W Sus* 1A **46**
Scayne's Hill. *W Sus* 3B **36**
School Green. *Essx* 1B **10**
Scotland End. *Oxon* 1A **4**
Seabrook. *Kent* 2B **40**
Seaford. *E Sus* 3C **47**
Seal. *Kent* 3D **27**
Seale. *Surr* 1A **34**
Seasalter. *Kent* 2A **30**
Seaview. *IOW* 3C **43**
Seawick. *Essx* 3B **12**
Sedlescombe. *E Sus* 1B **48**
Seer Green. *Buck* 2B **16**
Segensworth. *Hants* 2B **42**
Selborne. *Hants* 2B **33**

Selham. *W Sus* 3B **34**
Sellindge. *Kent* 2B **40**
Selling. *Kent* .3A **30**
Selmeston. *E Sus* 2D **47**
Selsdon. *G Lon* 2B **26**
Selsey. *W Sus* 3A **44**
Selsfield Common. *W Sus* 2B **36**
Selsted. *Kent* 1C **41**
Send. *Surr* 3C **25**
Send Marsh. *Surr* 3C **25**
Sennicotts. *W Sus* 2A **44**
Sevenoaks. *Kent* 3D **27**
Sevenoaks Weald. *Kent* 3D **27**
Sevington. *Kent* 1A **40**
Sewards End. *Essx* 1D **9**
Sewardstone. *Essx* 2B **18**
Sewardstonebury. *Essx* 2B **18**
Sewell. *C Beds* 2B **6**
Shabbington. *Buck* 1C **15**
Shackleford. *Surr* 1B **34**
Shadoxhurst. *Kent* 2D **39**
Shalden. *Hants* 1C **33**
Shalfleet. *IOW* 3A **42**
Shalford. *Essx* 2B **10**
Shalford. *Surr* 1C **35**
Shalford Green. *Essx* 2B **10**
Shalmsford Street. *Kent* 3A **30**
Shalstone. *Buck* 1C **5**
Shamley Green. *Surr* 1C **35**
Sharnal Street. *Medw* 1B **28**
Sharpenhoe. *C Beds* 1C **7**
Sharpthorne. *W Sus* 2B **36**
Shaw. *W Ber* 2A **22**
Shawford. *Hants* 3A **32**
Shedfield. *Hants* 1B **42**
Sheering. *Essx* 3D **9**
Sheerness. *Kent* 1D **29**
Sheerwater. *Surr* 2C **25**
Sheet. *Hants* 3D **33**
Sheffield Bottom. *W Ber* 2C **23**
Sheffield Green. *E Sus* 3C **37**
Shefford. *C Beds* 1D **7**
Shefford Woodlands. *W Ber* 1A **22**
Sheldwich. *Kent* 3A **30**
Sheldwich Lees. *Kent* 3A **30**
Shelley. *Suff* .1A **12**
Shellow Bowells. *Essx* 1A **20**
Shenfield. *Essx* 2A **20**
Shenington. *Oxon* 1A **4**
Shenley. *Herts* 1D **17**
Shenley Brook End. *Mil* 1A **6**
Shenleybury. *Herts* 1D **17**
Shenley Church End. *Mil* 1A **6**
Shephall. *Herts* 2A **8**
Shepherd's Bush. *G Lon* 3A **18**
Shepherd's Green. *Oxon* 3D **15**
Shepherdswell. *Kent* 1C **41**
Shepperton. *Surr* 2C **25**
Shepway. *Kent* 3B **28**
Sherborne St John. *Hants* 3C **23**
Shere. *Surr* 1C **35**
Sherfield on Loddon. *Hants* 3C **23**
Shermanbury. *W Sus* 1A **46**
Shide. *IOW* .3B **42**
Shillingford. *Oxon* 2B **14**
Shillington. *C Beds* 1D **7**
Shinfield. *Wok* 2D **23**
Shingle Street. *Suff* 1D **13**
Shipbourne. *Kent* 3D **27**
Shiplake. *Oxon* 1D **23**
Shipley. *W Sus* 3D **35**
Shipley Bridge. *Surr* 1B **36**
Shippon. *Oxon* 2A **14**
Shipton. *Buck* 2D **5**
Shipton Green. *W Sus* 3A **44**
Shipton-on-Cherwell. *Oxon* 3A **4**
Shirburn. *Oxon* 2C **15**
Shirkoak. *Kent* 2D **39**
Shirley. *Sotn* 1A **42**
Shirrell Heath. *Hants* 1B **42**
Shoeburyness. *S'end* 3D **21**
Sholden. *Kent* 3D **31**
Sholing. *Sotn* 1A **42**
Shoreditch. *G Lon* 3B **18**
Shoreham. *Kent* 2D **27**
Shoreham-by-Sea. *W Sus* 2A **46**
Shorne. *Kent* 1A **28**
Shorne Ridgeway. *Kent* 1A **28**
Shortbridge. *E Sus* 3C **37**
Shortgate. *E Sus* 1C **47**
Shotgate. *Essx* 2B **20**
Shotley. *Suff* .1C **13**
Shotley Gate. *Suff* 1C **13**
Shottenden. *Kent* 3A **30**
Shottermill. *Surr* 2A **34**
Shreding Green. *Buck* 3C **17**
Shripney. *W Sus* 2B **44**
Shrub End. *Essx* 2D **11**
Shurlock Row. *Wind* 1A **24**
Shutford. *Oxon* 1A **4**
Sibertswold. *Kent* 1C **41**
Sibford Ferris. *Oxon* 1A **4**
Sibford Gower. *Oxon* 1A **4**
Sible Hedingham. *Essx* 1B **10**
Sidcup. *G Lon* 1C **27**
Sidlesham. *W Sus* 3A **44**
Sidley. *E Sus* .2B **48**
Sidlow. *Surr* .1A **36**

Silchester. *Hants* 2C **23**
Silsoe. *C Beds* 1C **7**
Silver End. *Essx* 3C **11**
Sindlesham. *Wok* 2D **23**
Singleborough. *Buck* 1D **5**
Singleton. *Kent* 1D **39**
Singleton. *W Sus* 1A **44**
Singlewell. *Kent* 1A **28**
Sinkhurst Green. *Kent* 1C **39**
Sipson. *G Lon* 1C **25**
Sissinghurst. *Kent* 2B **38**
Sittingbourne. *Kent* 2D **29**
Skirmett. *Buck* 2D **15**
Skittle Green. *Buck* 1D **15**
Skye Green. *Essx* 2C **11**
Slade End. *Oxon* 2B **14**
Slade Green. *G Lon* 1D **27**
Slade, The. *W Ber* 2B **22**
Slapton. *Buck* 2B **6**
Slaugham. *W Sus* 3A **36**
Sleaford. *Hants* 2A **34**
Slindon. *W Sus* 2B **44**
Slinfold. *W Sus* 2D **35**
Slip End. *C Beds* 3C **7**
Slough. *Slo* 3B **16**
Slough Green. *W Sus* 3A **36**
Small Dole. *W Sus* 1A **46**
Smallfield. *Surr* 1B **36**
Small Hythe. *Kent* 2C **39**
Smannell. *Hants* 1A **32**
Smarden. *Kent* 1C **39**
Smarden Bell. *Kent* 1C **39**
Smart's Hill. *Kent* 1D **37**
Smeeth. *Kent* 2A **40**
Smith's Green. *Essx* 2D **9**
Smyth's Green. *Essx* 3D **11**
Snargate. *Kent* 3D **39**
Snave. *Kent* 3A **40**
Snodland. *Kent* 2A **28**
Soake. *Hants* 1C **43**
Soberton. *Hants* 1C **43**
Soberton Heath. *Hants* 1C **43**
Soldridge. *Hants* 2C **33**
Solent Breezes. *Hants* 2B **42**
Sole Street. *Kent* 2A **28**
(nr. Meopham)
Sole Street. *Kent* 1A **40**
(nr. Waltham)
Somerley. *W Sus* 3A **44**
Somerton. *Oxon* 2A **4**
Sompting. *W Sus* 2D **45**
Sonning. *Wok* 1D **23**
Sonning Common. *Oxon* 3D **15**
Sonning Eye. *Oxon* 1D **23**
Soulbury. *Buck* 2A **6**
Souldern. *Oxon* 1B **4**
Southall. *G Lon* 1D **25**
South Ambersham. *W Sus* 3B **34**
Southampton. *Sotn* ....1A **42 & 57**
Southampton International Airport.
Hants 1A **42**
South Ascot. *Wind* 2B **24**
South Baddesley. *Hants* 3A **42**
South Benfleet. *Essx* 3B **20**
South Bersted. *W Sus* 2B **44**
Southborough. *Kent* 1D **37**
Southbourne. *W Sus* 2D **43**
Southchurch. *S'end* 3D **21**
South Common. *E Sus* 1B **46**
Southcourt. *Buck* 3A **6**
South Darenth. *Kent* 2D **27**
South Downs. *W Sus* 2A **46**
Southease. *E Sus* 2C **47**
South End. *W Ber* 1B **22**
Southend (London) Airport. *Essx* 3C **21**
Southend-on-Sea. *S'end* 3C **21**
Southernden. *Kent* 1C **39**
Southey Green. *Essx* 1B **10**
South Fambridge. *Essx* 2C **21**
South Fawley. *W Ber* 3A **14**
Southfleet. *Kent* 1A **28**
Southgate. *G Lon* 2B **18**
South Godstone. *Surr* 1B **36**
South Green. *Essx* 2A **20**
(nr. Billericay)
South Green. *Essx* 3A **12**
(nr. Colchester)
South Green. *Kent* 2C **29**
South Hanningfield. *Essx* 2B **20**
South Harting. *W Sus* 1D **43**
South Hayling. *Hants* 3D **43**
South Heath. *Buck* 1B **16**
South Heath. *Essx* 3B **12**
South Heighton. *E Sus* 2C **47**
South Hinksey. *Oxon* 1B **14**
South Holmwood. *Surr* 1D **35**
South Hornchurch. *G Lon* 3D **19**
Southill. *C Beds* 1D **7**
Southington. *Hants* 1B **32**
South Lancing. *W Sus* 2D **45**
South Leigh. *Oxon* 1A **14**
South Malling. *E Sus* 1C **47**
South Mimms. *Herts* 1A **18**
Southminster. *Essx* 2D **21**
Southmoor. *Oxon* 2A **14**
South Moreton. *Oxon* 3B **14**
South Mundham. *W Sus* 2A **44**

South Newington. *Oxon* 1A **4**
South Norwood. *G Lon* 2B **26**
South Nutfield. *Surr* 1B **36**
South Ockendon. *Thur* 3D **19**
South Oxhey. *Herts* 2D **17**
Southrope. *Hants* 1C **33**
South Stifford. *Thur* 1D **27**
South Stoke. *Oxon* 3B **14**
South Stoke. *W Sus* 1C **45**
South Street. *E Sus* 1B **46**
South Street. *Kent* 3A **30**
(nr. Faversham)
South Street. *Kent* 2B **30**
(nr. Whitstable)
South Town. *Hants* 2C **33**
South Warnborough. *Hants* 1D **33**
Southwater. *W Sus* 3D **35**
Southwater Street. *W Sus* 3D **35**
South Weald. *Essx* 2D **19**
South Weston. *Oxon* 2D **15**
Southwick. *Hants* 2C **43**
Southwick. *W Sus* 2A **46**
South Wonston. *Hants* 2A **32**
South Woodham Ferrers. *Essx* 2C **21**
Sparrow's Green. *E Sus* 2A **38**
Sparsholt. *Hants* 2A **32**
Sparsholt. *Oxon* 3A **14**
Spear Hill. *W Sus* 1D **45**
Speen. *Buck* 2A **16**
Speen. *W Ber* 2A **22**
Speldhurst. *Kent* 1D **37**
Spellbrook. *Herts* 3C **9**
Spelsbury. *Oxon* 2A **4**
Spencers Wood. *Wok* 2D **23**
Spithurst. *E Sus* 1C **47**
Spreakley. *Surr* 1A **34**
Spring Vale. *IOW* 3C **43**
Stadhampton. *Oxon* 2C **15**
Stagden Cross. *Essx* 3A **10**
Staines-Upon-Thames. *Surr* 1C **25**
Stakes. *Hants* 2C **43**
Stalisfield Green. *Kent* 3D **29**
Stambourne. *Essx* 1B **10**
Stanborough. *Herts* 3A **8**
Stanbridge. *C Beds* 2B **6**
Standen. *Kent* 1C **39**
Standen Street. *Kent* 2C **39**
Standford. *Hants* 2A **34**
Standlake. *Oxon* 1A **14**
Standon. *Hants* 3A **32**
Standon. *Herts* 2B **8**
Standon Green End. *Herts* 3B **8**
Standford. *C Beds* 1D **7**
Stanford. *Kent* 2B **40**
Stanford Dingley. *W Ber* 1B **22**
Stanford in the Vale. *Oxon* 2A **14**
Stanford-le-Hope. *Thur* 3A **20**
Stanford Rivers. *Essx* 1D **19**
Stanmer. *Brig* 2B **46**
Stanmore. *G Lon* 2D **17**
Stanmore. *Hants* 3A **32**
Stanmore. *W Ber* 1A **22**
Stanstead Abbotts. *Herts* 3B **8**
Stansted. *Kent* 2A **28**
Stansted (London) Airport.
Essx ....2D **9 & 59**
Stansted Mountfitchet. *Essx* 2D **9**
Stanton Harcourt. *Oxon* 1A **14**
Stanton St John. *Oxon* 1B **14**
Stanway. *Essx* 2D **11**
Stanwell. *Surr* 1C **25**
Stanwell Moor. *Surr* 1C **25**
Staple. *Kent* 3C **31**
Staplecross. *E Sus* 3B **38**
Staplefield. *W Sus* 3A **36**
Stapleford. *Herts* 3B **8**
Stapleford Abbotts. *Essx* 2D **19**
Stapleford Tawney. *Essx* 2D **19**
Staplehurst. *Kent* 1B **38**
Staplers. *IOW* 3B **42**
Starling's Green. *Essx* 1C **9**
Start Hill. *Essx* 2D **9**
Stebbing. *Essx* 2A **10**
Stebbing Green. *Essx* 2A **10**
Stedham. *W Sus* 3A **34**
Steel Cross. *E Sus* 2D **37**
Steep. *Hants* 3D **33**
Steeple. *Essx* 1D **21**
Steeple Aston. *Oxon* 2A **4**
Steeple Barton. *Oxon* 2A **4**
Steeple Bumpstead. *Essx* 1A **10**
Steeple Claydon. *Buck* 2C **5**
Steeple Morden. *Cambs* 1A **8**
Stelling Minnis. *Kent* 1B **40**
Stepney. *G Lon* 3B **18**
Steppingley. *C Beds* 1C **7**
Stevenage. *Herts* 2A **8**
Steventon. *Hants* 1B **32**
Steventon. *Oxon* 2A **14**
Steventon End. *Cambs* 1A **10**
Stewartby. *Bed* 1C **7**
Stewkley. *Buck* 2A **6**
Stewkley Dean. *Buck* 2A **6**
Steyning. *W Sus* 1D **45**
Stickling Green. *Essx* 1C **9**
Stisted. *Essx* 2B **10**

Stock. *Essx* 2A **20**
Stockbridge. *Hants* 2A **32**
Stockbury. *Kent* 2C **29**
Stockcross. *W Ber* 2A **22**
Stocker's Head. *Kent* 3D **29**
Stocking Green. *Essx* 1D **9**
Stocking Pelham. *Herts* 2C **9**
Stocks, The. *Kent* 3D **39**
Stockstreet. *Essx* 2C **11**
Stodmarsh. *Kent* 2C **31**
Stoke. *Hants* 3A **22**
(nr. Andover)
Stoke. *Hants* 2D **43**
(nr. South Hayling)
Stoke. *Medw* 1C **29**
Stoke by Clare. *Suff* 1B **10**
Stoke-by-Nayland. *Suff* 1D **11**
Stoke Charity. *Hants* 2A **32**
Stoke D'Abernon. *Surr* 3D **25**
Stoke Hammond. *Buck* 2A **6**
Stoke Lyne. *Oxon* 2B **4**
Stoke Mandeville. *Buck* 3A **6**
Stokenchurch. *Buck* 2D **15**
Stoke Newington. *G Lon* 3B **18**
Stoke Poges. *Buck* 3B **16**
Stoke Row. *Oxon* 3C **15**
Stoke Talmage. *Oxon* 2C **15**
Stondon Massey. *Essx* 1D **19**
Stone. *Buck* 3D **5**
Stone. *Kent* 1D **27**
Stonebridge. *Kent* 1D **35**
Stone Cross. *E Sus* 2A **48**
Stone Cross. *Kent* 2D **37**
Stonegate. *E Sus* 3A **38**
Stone Hill. *Kent* 2A **40**
Stone in Oxney. *Kent* 3D **39**
Stoner Hill. *Hants* 3D **33**
Stonesfield. *Oxon* 3A **4**
Stones Green. *Essx* 2B **12**
Stone Street. *Kent* 3D **27**
Stoneyhills. *Essx* 2D **21**
Stonor. *Oxon* 3D **15**
Stony Stratford. *Mil* 1D **5**
Stopham. *W Sus* 1C **45**
Stopsley. *Lutn* 2D **7**
Storrington. *W Sus* 1C **45**
Stotfold. *C Beds* 1A **8**
Stoughton. *Surr* 3B **24**
Stoughton. *W Sus* 1A **44**
Stow Maries. *Essx* 2C **21**
Stowting. *Kent* 1B **40**
Stratfield Mortimer. *W Ber* 2C **23**
Stratfield Saye. *Hants* 2C **23**
Stratfield Turgis. *Hants* 3C **23**
Stratford. *G Lon* 3B **18**
Stratford St Mary. *Suff* 1A **12**
Stratton Audley. *Oxon* 2C **5**
Streat. *E Sus* 1B **46**
Streatham. *G Lon* 1B **26**
Streatley. *C Beds* 2C **7**
Streatley. *W Ber* 3B **14**
Street End. *Kent* 3B **30**
Street End. *W Sus* 3A **44**
Strethall. *Essx* 1C **9**
Strood. *Kent* 2C **39**
Strood. *Medw* 2B **28**
Strood Green. *Surr* 1A **36**
Strood Green. *W Sus* 2B **35**
(nr. Billingshurst)
Strood Green. *W Sus* 2D **35**
(nr. Horsham)
Stroud. *Hants* 3D **33**
Stroud Green. *Essx* 2C **21**
Stubbington. *Hants* 2B **42**
Stubb's Cross. *Kent* 3D **39**
Studham. *C Beds* 3C **7**
Stunts Green. *E Sus* 1A **48**
Sturmer. *Essx* 1A **10**
Sturry. *Kent* 2B **30**
Stutton. *Suff* 1B **12**
Sutton. *Buck* 1C **25**
Sutton. *E Sus* 3C **47**
Sutton. *G Lon* 2A **26**
Sutton. *Kent* 1D **41**
Sutton. *Oxon* 1A **14**
Sutton. *W Sus* 1B **44**
Sutton Abinger. *Surr* 1D **35**
Sutton at Hone. *Kent* 2D **27**
Sutton Courtenay. *Oxon* 2B **14**
Sutton Green. *Surr* 3C **25**
Sutton Scotney. *Hants* 2A **32**

Sutton Valence. *Kent* 1C **39**
Swalcliffe. *Oxon* 1A **4**
Swalecliffe. *Kent* 2B **30**
Swallowfield. *Wok* 2D **23**
Swampton. *Hants* 3A **22**
Swanbourne. *Buck* 2A **6**
Swanley. *Kent* 2D **27**
Swanmore. *Hants* 1B **42**
Swanscombe. *Kent* 1D **27**
Swan Street. *Essx* 2C **11**
Swanton Street. *Kent* 3C **29**
Swanwick. *Hants* 2B **42**
Swarraton. *Hants* 2B **32**
Swaythling. *Sotn* 1A **42**
Swerford. *Oxon* 1A **4**
Swiftsden. *E Sus* 3B **38**
Swinford. *Oxon* 1A **14**
Swingfield Minnis. *Kent* 1C **41**
Swingfield Street. *Kent* 1C **41**
Sydenham. *G Lon* 1B **26**
Sydenham. *Oxon* 1D **15**
Sydmonton. *Hants* 3A **22**
Syresham. *Nptn* 1C **5**

T

Tackley. *Oxon* 2A **4**
Tadley. *Hants* 2C **23**
Tadmarton. *Oxon* 1A **4**
Tadworth. *Surr* 3A **26**
Takeley. *Essx* 2D **9**
Takeley Street. *Essx* 2D **9**
Tandridge. *Surr* 3B **26**
Tangmere. *W Sus* 2B **44**
Tankerton. *Kent* 2B **30**
Taplow. *Buck* 3B **16**
Tarpots. *Essx* 3B **20**
Tarring Neville. *E Sus* 2C **47**
Taston. *Oxon* 2A **4**
Tatling End. *Buck* 3C **17**
Tatsfield. *Surr* 3C **27**
Tattingstone. *Suff* 1B **12**
Tattingstone White Horse. *Suff* 1B **12**
Taverners Green. *Essx* 3D **9**
Tebworth. *C Beds* 2B **6**
Teddington. *G Lon* 1D **25**
Telham. *E Sus* 1B **48**
Telscombe. *E Sus* 2C **47**
Telscombe Cliffs. *E Sus* 2B **46**
Temple Ewell. *Kent* 1C **41**
Templeton. *W Ber* 2A **22**
Tendring. *Essx* 2B **12**
Tendring Green. *Essx* 2B **12**
Tenterden. *Kent* 2C **39**
Terling. *Essx* 3B **10**
Terrick. *Buck* 1A **16**
Teston. *Kent* 3B **28**
Testwood. *Hants* 1A **42**
Tetsworth. *Oxon* 1C **15**
Tewin. *Herts* 3A **8**
Teynham. *Kent* 2D **29**
Teynham Street. *Kent* 2D **29**
Thakeham. *W Sus* 1D **45**
Thame. *Oxon* 1D **15**
Thames Ditton. *Surr* 2D **25**
Thames Haven. *Thur* 3B **20**
Thamesmead. *G Lon* 3C **19**
Thamesport. *Kent* 1C **29**
Thamesport. *Medw* 1C **29**
Thanington Without. *Kent* 3B **30**
Thatcham. *W Ber* 2B **22**
Thaxted. *Essx* 1A **10**
Theale. *W Ber* 1C **23**
Thenford. *Nptn* 1B **4**
Therfield. *Herts* 1B **8**
Theydon Bois. *Essx* 2C **19**
Thong. *Kent* 1A **28**
Thorington Street. *Suff* 1A **12**
Thorley. *Herts* 3C **9**
Thorley Street. *Herts* 3C **9**
Thorley Street. *IOW* 3A **42**
Thornborough. *Buck* 1D **5**
Thorncombe Street. *Surr* 1B **34**
Thornhill. *Sotn* 1A **42**
Thornton. *Buck* 1D **5**
Thornton Heath. *G Lon* 2B **26**
Thornwood Common. *Essx* 1C **19**
Thorpe. *Surr* 2C **25**
Thorpe Bay. *S'end* 3D **21**
Thorpe Common. *Suff* 1C **13**
Thorpe Green. *Essx* 2B **12**
Thorpe-le-Soken. *Essx* 2B **12**
Thorrington. *Essx* 2A **12**
Three Bridges. *W Sus* 2A **36**
Three Chimneys. *Kent* 2C **39**
Three Cups Corner. *E Sus* 3A **38**
Three Leg Cross. *E Sus* 3A **38**
Three Mile Cross. *Wok* 2D **23**
Three Oaks. *E Sus* 1C **49**
Throcking. *Herts* 1B **8**
Throwley. *Kent* 3D **29**
Throwley Forstal. *Kent* 3D **29**
Thrupp. *Oxon* 3A **4**
Thundersley. *Essx* 3B **20**
Thundridge. *Herts* 3B **8**
Thurnham. *Kent* 3C **29**

Thursley. *Surr* 2B **34**
Ticehurst. *E Sus* 2A **38**
Tichborne. *Hants* 2B **32**
Tiddington. *Oxon* 1C **15**
Tidebrook. *E Sus* 3A **38**
Tidmarsh. *W Ber* 1C **23**
Tilbury. *Thur* 1A **28**
Tilbury Green. *Essx* 1B **10**
Tilbury Juxta Clare. *Essx* 1B **10**
Tilehurst. *Read* 1C **23**
Tilford. *Surr* 1A **34**
Tilgate Forest Row. *W Sus* 2A **36**
Tillingham. *Essx* 1D **21**
Tillington. *W Sus* 3B **34**
Tilmanstone. *Kent* 3D **31**
Tilsworth. *C Beds* 2B **6**
Timsbury. *Hants* 3A **32**
Tingewick. *Buck* 1C **5**
Tingrith. *C Beds* 1C **7**
Tinsley Green. *W Sus* 2A **36**
Tiptree. *Essx* 3C **11**
Tiptree Heath. *Essx* 3C **11**
Tisman's Common. *W Sus* 2C **35**
Titchfield. *Hants* 2B **42**
Titsey. *Surr* 3C **27**
Toddington. *C Beds* 2C **7**
Tokers Green. *Oxon* 1D **23**
Tollesbury. *Essx* 3D **11**
Tolleshunt D'Arcy. *Essx* 3D **11**
Tolleshunt Knights. *Essx* 3D **11**
Tolleshunt Major. *Essx* 3D **11**
Tolworth. *G Lon* 2D **25**
Tonbridge. *Kent* 1D **37**
Tongham. *Surr* 1A **34**
Tonwell. *Herts* 3B **8**
Toot Baldon. *Oxon* 1B **14**
Toot Hill. *Essx* 1D **19**
Toot Hill. *Hants* 1A **42**
Toppesfield. *Essx* 1B **10**
Tortington. *W Sus* 2C **45**
Tottenham. *G Lon* 2B **18**
Totteridge. *G Lon* 2A **18**
Totternhoe. *C Beds* 2B **6**
Totton. *Hants* 1A **42**
Touchen-end. *Wind* 1A **24**
Tower Hill. *W Sus* 3D **35**
Towersey. *Oxon* 1D **15**
Town Littleworth. *E Sus* 1C **47**
Town Row. *E Sus* 2D **37**
Towns End. *Hants* 3B **22**
Townsend. *Herts* 1D **17**
Toy's Hill. *Kent* 3C **27**
Trash Green. *W Ber* 2C **23**
Treyford. *W Sus* 1A **44**
Trimley Lower Street. *Suff* 1C **13**
Trimley St Martin. *Suff* 1C **13**
Trimley St Mary. *Suff* 1C **13**
Tring. *Herts* 3B **6**
Trottiscliffe. *Kent* 2A **28**
Trotton. *W Sus* 3A **34**
Trowley Bottom. *Herts* 3C **7**
Trumps Green. *Surr* 2B **24**
Tubney. *Oxon* 2A **14**
Tudeley. *Kent* 1A **38**
Tuesley. *Surr* 1B **34**
Tufton. *Hants* 1A **32**
Tumbler's Green. *Essx* 2C **11**
Tunbridge Wells, Royal. *Kent* . .2D **37**
Tunstall. *Kent* 2C **29**
Tunworth. *Hants* 1C **33**
Turgis Green. *Hants* 3C **23**
Turkey Island. *Hants* 1B **42**
Turners Hill. *W Sus* 2B **36**
Turnford. *Herts* 1B **18**
Turville. *Buck* 2D **15**
Turville Heath. *Buck* 2D **15**
Turweston. *Buck* 1C **5**
Tutts Clump. *W Ber* 1B **22**
Twickenham. *G Lon* 1D **25**
Twineham. *W Sus* 3A **36**
Twinstead. *Essx* 1C **11**
Twinstead Green. *Essx* 1C **11**
Twyford. *Buck* 2C **5**
Twyford. *Hants* 3A **32**
Twyford. *Wok* 1D **23**
Tye. *Hants* 2D **43**
Tye Green. *Essx* 2D **9**
(nr. Bishop's Stortford)
Tye Green. *Essx* 2B **10**
(nr. Braintree)
Tye Green. *Essx* 1D **9**
(nr. Saffron Walden)
Tyler Hill. *Kent* 2B **30**
Tylers Green. *Buck* 2A **16**
Tyler's Green. *Essx* 1D **19**

U

Uckfield. *E Sus* 3C **37**
Udimore. *E Sus* 1C **49**
Ufton Nervet. *W Ber* 2C **23**
Ugley. *Essx* 2D **9**
Ugley Green. *Essx* 2D **9**
Ulcombe. *Kent* 1C **39**
Ulting. *Essx* 1C **21**
Underriver. *Kent* 3D **27**

Union Street. *E Sus* 2B **38**
Upchurch. *Kent* 2C **29**
Upham. *Hants* 3B **32**
Uplees. *Kent* 2D **29**
Up Marden. *W Sus* 1D **43**
Upminster. *G Lon* 3D **19**
Up Nately. *Hants* 3C **23**
Upper Arncott. *Oxon* 3C **5**
Upper Astrop. *Nptn* 1B **4**
Upper Basildon. *W Ber* 1B **22**
Upper Beeding. *W Sus* 1D **45**
Upper Bucklebury. *W Ber* 2B **22**
Upper Bullington. *Hants* 1A **32**
Upper Clatford. *Hants* 1A **32**
Upper Cokeham. *W Sus* 2D **45**
Upper Common. *Hants* 1C **33**
Upper Dicker. *E Sus* 2D **47**
Upper Dovercourt. *Essx* 1C **13**
Upper Dunsley. *Herts* 3B **6**
Upper Enham. *Hants* 1A **32**
Upper Farringdon. *Hants* 2D **33**
Upper Froyle. *Hants* 1D **33**
Upper Gravenhurst. *C Beds* 1D **7**
Upper Green. *Essx* 1C **9**
Upper Green. *W Ber* 2A **22**
Upper Hale. *Surr* 1A **34**
Upper Halliford. *Surr* 2C **25**
Upper Halling. *Medw* 2A **28**
Upper Hardres Court. *Kent* 3B **30**
Upper Hartfield. *E Sus* 2C **37**
Upper Heyford. *Oxon* 2A **4**
Upper Layham. *Suff* 1A **12**
Upper North Dean. *Buck* 2A **16**
Upper Norwood. *W Sus* 1B **44**
Upper Shelton. *C Beds* 1B **6**
Upper Stondon. *C Beds* 1D **7**
Upper Street. *Suff* 1B **12**
Upper Sundon. *C Beds* 2C **7**
Upperton. *W Sus* 3B **34**
Upper Tooting. *G Lon* 1A **26**
Upper Upnor. *Medw* 1B **28**
Upper Weald. *Mil* 1A **6**
Upper Wellingham. *E Sus* 1C **47**
Upper Wield. *Hants* 2C **33**
Upper Winchendon. *Buck* 3D **5**
Upper Wootton. *Hants* 3B **22**
Upshire. *Essx* 1C **19**
Up Somborne. *Hants* 2A **32**
Upstreet. *Kent* 2C **31**
Upton. *Buck* 3D **5**
Upton. *Hants* 1A **42**
(nr. Andover)
Upton. *Hants* 3B **22**
(nr. Southampton)
Upton. *IOW* 3B **42**
Upton. *Oxon* 3B **14**
Upton. *Slo* 1B **24**
Upton End. *C Beds* 1D **7**
Upton Grey. *Hants* 1C **33**
Upwaltham. *W Sus* 1B **44**
Upwick Green. *Herts* 2C **9**
Uxbridge. *G Lon* 3C **17**

V

Valley End. *Surr* 2B **24**
Vange. *Essx* 3B **20**
Vernham Street. *Hants* 3A **22**
Vigo Village. *Kent* 2A **28**
Vinehall Street. *E Sus* 3B **38**
Vine's Cross. *E Sus* 1D **47**
Virginia Water. *Surr* 2B **24**

W

Waddesdon. *Buck* 3D **5**
Wadesmill. *Herts* 3B **8**
Wadhurst. *E Sus* 2A **38**
Wadwick. *Hants* 3A **22**
Wainscott. *Medw* 1B **28**
Wakes Colne. *Essx* 2C **11**
Walberton. *W Sus* 2B **44**
Walderslade. *Medw* 2B **28**
Walderton. *W Sus* 1D **43**
Waldron. *E Sus* 1D **47**
Walkern. *Herts* 2A **8**
Wallands Park. *E Sus* 1C **47**
Wallcrouch. *E Sus* 2A **38**
Wallend. *Medw* 1C **29**
Wallingford. *Oxon* 3C **15**
Wallington. *G Lon* 2A **26**
Wallington. *Hants* 2B **42**
Wallington. *Herts* 1A **8**
Walliswood. *Surr* 2D **35**
Walmer. *Kent* 3D **31**
Walsworth. *Herts* 1D **7**
Walter's Ash. *Buck* 2A **16**
Waltham. *Kent* 1B **40**
Waltham Abbey. *Essx* 1B **18**
Waltham Chase. *Hants* 1B **42**
Waltham Cross. *Herts* 1B **18**
Waltham St Lawrence. *Wind* 1A **24**
Waltham's Cross. *Essx* 1A **10**
Walthamstow. *G Lon* 3B **18**
Walton. *Mil* 1A **6**

Walton. *Suff* 1C **13**
Walton-on-Thames. *Surr* 2D **25**
Walton on the Hill. *Surr* 3A **26**
Walton-on-the-Naze. *Essx* 2C **13**
Wanborough. *Surr* 1B **34**
Wandsworth. *G Lon* 1A **26**
Wannock. *E Sus* 2D **47**
Wanshurst Green. *Kent* 1B **38**
Wanstead. *G Lon* 3C **19**
Wantage. *Oxon* 3A **14**
Warbleton. *E Sus* 1A **48**
Warblington. *Hants* 2D **43**
Warborough. *Oxon* 2B **14**
Warden. *Kent* 1A **30**
Wardhedges. *C Beds* 1C **7**
Wardley. *W Sus* 3A **34**
Ware. *Herts* 3B **8**
Ware. *Kent* 2C **31**
Warehorne. *Kent* 2D **39**
Wareside. *Herts* 3B **8**
Warfield. *Brac* 1A **24**
Wargrave. *Wok* 1D **23**
Warkworth. *Nptn* 1A **4**
Warlingham. *Surr* 3B **26**
Warminghurst. *W Sus* 1D **45**
Warners End. *Herts* 1C **17**
Warnford. *Hants* 3C **33**
Warnham. *W Sus* 2D **35**
Warningcamp. *W Sus* 2C **45**
Warninglid. *W Sus* 3A **36**
Warren Corner. *Hants* 1A **4**
(nr. Aldershot)
Warren Corner. *Hants* 3D **33**
(nr. Petersfield)
Warren Row. *Wind* 3A **16**
Warren Street. *Kent* 3D **29**
Warsash. *Hants* 2A **42**
Wartling. *E Sus* 2A **48**
Warwick Wold. *Surr* 3B **26**
Washbrook. *Suff* 1B **12**
Wash Common. *W Ber* 2A **22**
Washington. *W Sus* 1D **45**
Wasp Green. *Surr* 1B **36**
Waterbeach. *W Sus* 2A **44**
Water End. *C Beds* 1C **7**
Water End. *Essx* 1D **9**
Water End. *Herts* 1A **18**
(nr. Hatfield)
Water End. *Herts* 1D **17**
(nr. Hemel Hempstead)
Waterford. *Herts* 3B **8**
Wateringbury. *Kent* 3A **28**
Waterlooville. *Hants* 2C **43**
Watermead. *Buck* 3A **6**
Waterperry. *Oxon* 1C **15**
Watersfield. *W Sus* 1C **45**
Waterside. *Buck* 1B **16**
Waterstock. *Oxon* 1C **15**
Water Stratford. *Buck* 1C **5**
Watford. *Herts* 2C **17**
Watlington. *Oxon* 2C **15**
Watton at Stone. *Herts* 3A **8**
Wavendon. *Mil* 1B **6**
Waverley. *Surr* 1A **34**
Wealdstone. *G Lon* 3D **17**
Weedon. *Buck* 3A **6**
Weeke. *Hants* 2A **32**
Weeley. *Essx* 2B **12**
Weeley Heath. *Essx* 2B **12**
Welford. *W Ber* 1A **22**
Welham Green. *Herts* 1A **18**
Well. *Hants* 1D **33**
Well Hill. *Kent* 2C **27**
Wellhouse. *W Ber* 1B **22**
Welling. *G Lon* 1C **27**
Wellow. *IOW* 3A **42**
Wellpond Green. *Herts* 2C **9**
Welwyn. *Herts* 3A **8**
Welwyn Garden City. *Herts* 3A **8**
Wembley. *G Lon* 3D **17**
Wendens Ambo. *Essx* 1D **9**
Wendlebury. *Oxon* 3B **4**
Wendover. *Buck* 1A **16**
Wennington. *G Lon* 3D **19**
Wepham. *W Sus* 2C **45**
West Ashling. *W Sus* 2A **44**
Westbere. *Kent* 2B **30**
West Bergholt. *Essx* 2D **11**
West Blatchington. *Brig* 2A **46**
Westbourne. *W Sus* 2D **43**
West Brabourne. *Kent* 1A **40**
Westbrook. *Kent* 1D **31**
West Burton. *W Sus* 1C **45**
Westbury. *Buck* 1C **5**
West Byfleet. *Surr* 2C **25**
West Challow. *Oxon* 3A **14**
West Chiltington. *W Sus* 1C **45**
West Chiltington Common.
    W Sus 1C **45**
West Clandon. *Surr* 3C **25**
West Cliffe. *Kent* 1A **40**
Westcliff-on-Sea. *S'end* 3C **21**
Westcot. *Oxon* 3A **14**
Westcott. *Buck* 3D **5**
Westcott. *Surr* 1D **35**
Westcott Barton. *Oxon* 2A **4**
Westdean. *E Sus* 3D **47**
West Dean. *W Sus* 1A **44**

West Drayton. *G Lon* 1C **25**
West End. *G Lon* 3A **18**
West End. *Hants* 1A **42**
West End. *Herts* 1A **18**
West End. *Kent* 2B **30**
West End. *Surr* 2B **24**
West End Green. *Hants* 2C **23**
Westenhanger. *Kent* 2B **40**
Westergate. *W Sus* 2B **44**
Westerham. *Kent* 3C **27**
Westerton. *W Sus* 2A **44**
West Farleigh. *Kent* 3B **28**
Westfield. *E Sus* 1C **49**
Westgate on Sea. *Kent* 1D **31**
West Ginge. *Oxon* 3A **14**
West Green. *Hants* 3D **23**
West Grinstead. *W Sus* 3D **35**
West Hagbourne. *Oxon* 3B **14**
Westham. *E Sus* 2A **48**
West Ham. *G Lon* 3B **18**
Westhampnett. *W Sus* 2A **44**
West Hanney. *Oxon* 2A **14**
West Hanningfield. *Essx* 2B **20**
West Harting. *W Sus* 3D **33**
West Heath. *Hants* 3B **22**
(nr. Basingstoke)
West Heath. *Hants* 3A **24**
(nr. Farnborough)
West Hendred. *Oxon* 3A **14**
West Hill. *W Sus* 2B **36**
West Hoathly. *W Sus* 2B **36**
West Horndon. *Essx* 3A **20**
West Horsley. *Surr* 3C **25**
West Hougham. *Kent* 1C **41**
Westhumble. *Surr* 3D **25**
West Hyde. *Herts* 2C **17**
West Hythe. *Kent* 2B **40**
West Ilsley. *W Ber* 3A **14**
West Itchenor. *W Sus* 2A **44**
West Kingsdown. *Kent* 2D **27**
West Langdon. *Kent* 1D **41**
West Lavington. *W Sus* 3A **34**
West Leith. *Buck* 3B **6**
Westlington. *Buck* 3D **5**
West Malling. *Kent* 3A **28**
West Marden. *W Sus* 1D **43**
Westmarsh. *Kent* 2C **31**
West Meon. *Hants* 3C **33**
West Mersea. *Essx* 3A **12**
Westmeston. *E Sus* 1B **46**
Westmill. *Herts* 2B **8**
(nr. Buntingford)
Westmill. *Herts* 1D **7**
(nr. Hitchin)
Westminster. *G Lon* 1A **26**
West Molesey. *Surr* 2D **25**
West Norwood. *G Lon* 1B **26**
Weston. *Hants* 3D **33**
Weston. *Herts* 1A **8**
Weston. *W Ber* 1A **22**
Westoning. *C Beds* 1C **7**
Weston-on-the-Green. *Oxon* 3B **4**
Weston Patrick. *Hants* 1C **33**
Weston Turville. *Buck* 3A **6**
West Peckham. *Kent* 3A **28**
West Stoke. *W Sus* 2A **44**
West Stourmouth. *Kent* 2C **31**
West Stratton. *Hants* 1B **32**
West Street. *Kent* 3D **29**
West Thorney. *W Sus* 2D **43**
West Thurrock. *Thur* 1D **27**
West Tilbury. *Thur* 1A **28**
West Tisted. *Hants* 3C **33**
West Town. *Hants* 3D **43**
Westwell. *Kent* 1D **39**
Westwell Leacon. *Kent* 1D **39**
West Wickham. *G Lon* 2B **26**
West Wittering. *W Sus* 3D **43**
Westwood. *Kent* 2D **31**
West Woodhay. *W Ber* 2A **22**
West Worldham. *Hants* 2D **33**
West Worthing. *W Sus* 2D **45**
West Wycombe. *Buck* 2A **16**
Wethersfield. *Essx* 1B **10**
Wexham Street. *Buck* 3B **16**
Weybourne. *Surr* 1A **34**
Weybridge. *Surr* 2C **25**
Whaddon. *Buck* 1A **6**
Wharley End. *C Beds* 1B **6**
Whatlington. *E Sus* 1B **48**
Wheathampstead. *Herts* 3D **7**
Wheatley. *Hants* 1D **33**
Wheatley. *Oxon* 1B **14**
Wheelerstreet. *Surr* 1B **34**
Whelpley Hill. *Buck* 1B **16**
Wherstead. *Suff* 1B **12**
Wherwell. *Hants* 1A **32**
Whetsted. *Kent* 1A **38**
Whetstone. *G Lon* 2A **18**
Whippingham. *IOW* 3B **42**
Whipsnade. *C Beds* 3C **7**
Whistley Green. *Wok* 1D **23**
Whitchurch. *Buck* 3D **5**
Whitchurch. *Hants* 1A **32**
Whitchurch Hill. *Oxon* 1C **23**
Whitchurch-on-Thames. *Oxon* 1C **23**

Whiteash Green. *Essx* 1B **10**
White Colne. *Essx* 2C **11**
Whitehall. *Hants* 3D **23**
Whitehall. *W Sus* 3D **35**
Whitehill. *Hants* 2D **33**
Whiteley. *Hants* 1B **42**
Whiteley Village. *Surr* 2C **25**
Whitemans Green. *W Sus* 3B **36**
Whitenap. *Hants* 3A **32**
White Notley. *Essx* 3B **10**
Whiteoak Green. *Oxon* 3A **4**
White Roding. *Essx* 3D **9**
Whitesmith. *E Sus* 1D **47**
Whitestreet Green. *Suff* 1D **11**
White Waltham. *Wind* 1A **24**
Whitfield. *Kent* 1D **41**
Whitfield. *Nptn* 1C **5**
Whitstable. *Kent* 2B **30**
Whitway. *Hants* 3A **22**
Whitwell. *Herts* 2D **7**
Whyteleafe. *Surr* 3B **26**
Wichling. *Kent* 3D **29**
Wick. *W Sus* 2C **45**
Wicken. *Nptn* 1D **5**
Wicken Bonhunt. *Essx* 1C **9**
Wicker Street Green. *Suff* 1D **11**
Wickford. *Essx* 2B **20**
Wickham. *Hants* 1B **42**
Wickham. *W Ber* 1A **22**
Wickham Bishops. *Essx* 3C **11**
Wickhambreaux. *Kent* 3C **31**
Wickham Heath. *W Ber* 2A **22**
Wickham St Paul. *Essx* 1C **11**
Wick Hill. *Wok* 2D **23**
Widdington. *Essx* 1D **9**
Widford. *Essx* 1A **20**
Widford. *Herts* 3C **9**
Widmer End. *Buck* 2A **16**
Wiggens Green. *Essx* 1A **10**
Wigginton. *Herts* 3B **6**
Wigginton. *Oxon* 1A **4**
Wiggonholt. *W Sus* 1C **45**
Wigmore. *Medw* 2C **29**
Wildern. *Hants* 1A **42**
Wildhern. *Hants* 3A **22**
Willen. *Mil* 1A **6**
Willesborough. *Kent* 1A **40**
Willesborough Lees.
   Kent 1A **40**
Willesden. *G Lon* 3A **18**
Willey Green. *Surr* 3B **24**
Willian. *Herts* 1A **8**
Willingale. *Essx* 1D **19**
Willingdon. *E Sus* 2D **47**
Willows Green. *Essx* 3B **10**
Wilmington. *E Sus* 2D **47**
Wilmington. *Kent* 1D **27**

Wilsley Green. *Kent* 2B **38**
Wilstead. *Bed* 1C **7**
Wilstone. *Herts* 3B **6**
Wimbish. *Essx* 1D **9**
Wimbish Green. *Essx* 1A **10**
Wimbledon. *G Lon* 1A **26**
Winchelsea. *E Sus* 1D **49**
Winchelsea Beach.
   E Sus 1D **49**
Winchester. *Hants* . . . . . .3A **32 & 57**
Winchet Hill. *Kent* 1B **38**
Winchfield. *Hants* 3D **23**
Winchmore Hill. *Buck* 2B **16**
Winchmore Hill. *G Lon* 2B **18**
Windlesham. *Surr* 2B **24**
Windmill Hill. *E Sus* 1A **48**
Windsor. *Wind* . . . . .1B **24 & 57**
Wineham. *W Sus* 3A **36**
Wing. *Buck* 2A **6**
Wingfield. *C Beds* 2C **7**
Wingham. *Kent* 3C **31**
Wingmore. *Kent* 1B **40**
Wingrave. *Buck* 3A **6**
Winkfield. *Brac* 1B **24**
Winkfield Row. *Brac* 1A **24**
Winklebury. *Hants* 3C **23**
Winnersh. *Wok* 1D **23**
Winslade. *Hants* 1C **33**
Winslow. *Buck* 2D **5**
Winterbourne. *W Ber* 1A **22**
Winterbrook. *Oxon* 3C **15**
Winter Gardens. *Essx* 3B **20**
Winton. *E Sus* 2D **47**
Wisborough Green. *W Sus* 3C **35**
Wisley. *Surr* 3C **25**
Wissenden. *Kent* 1D **39**
Wiston. *W Sus* 1D **45**
Witham. *Essx* 3C **11**
Witherenden Hill. *E Sus* 3A **38**
Witheridge Hill. *Oxon* 3C **15**
Withermarsh Green. *Suff* 1A **12**
Withyham. *E Sus* 2C **37**
Witley. *Surr* 1B **34**
Wittersham. *Kent* 3D **39**
Wivelrod. *Hants* 2C **33**
Wivelsfield. *E Sus* 3B **36**
Wivelsfield Green. *E Sus* 1B **46**
Wivenhoe. *Essx* 2A **12**
Wix. *Essx* 2B **12**
Wixoe. *Suff* 1B **10**
Woburn. *C Beds* 1B **6**
Woburn Sands. *Mil* 1B **6**
Woking. *Surr* 3C **25**
Wokingham. *Wok* 2A **24**
Woldingham. *Surr* 3B **26**
Wolvercote. *Oxon* 1A **14**

Wolverton. *Hants* 3B **22**
Wolverton. *Mil* 1A **6**
Wolverton Common. *Hants* 3B **22**
Womenswold. *Kent* 3C **31**
Wonersh. *Surr* 1C **35**
Wonston. *Hants* 2A **32**
Wooburn. *Buck* 3B **16**
Wooburn Green. *Buck* 3B **16**
Woodchurch. *Kent* 2D **39**
Woodcote. *Oxon* 3C **15**
Woodcott. *Hants* 3A **22**
Woodeaton. *Oxon* 3B **4**
Wood End. *Herts* 2B **8**
Woodend. *W Sus* 2A **44**
Woodend Green. *Essx* 2D **9**
Woodfield. *Oxon* 2B **4**
Woodford. *G Lon* 2B **18**
Woodford Green. *G Lon* 2C **19**
Woodgate. *W Sus* 2B **44**
Wood Green. *G Lon* 2A **18**
Woodgreen. *Oxon* 3A **4**
Woodham. *Surr* 2C **25**
Woodham Ferrers. *Essx* 2B **20**
Woodham Mortimer. *Essx* 1C **21**
Woodham Walter. *Essx* 1C **21**
Woodingdean. *Brig* 2B **46**
Woodlands. *Kent* 2D **27**
Woodlands Park. *Wind* 1A **24**
Woodley. *Wok* 1D **23**
Woodmancote. *W Sus* 2D **43**
   (nr. Chichester)
Woodmancote. *W Sus* 1A **46**
   (nr. Henfield)
Woodmancott. *Hants* 1B **32**
Woodmansgreen. *W Sus* 3A **34**
Woodmansterne. *Surr* 3A **26**
Woodnesborough. *Kent* 3D **31**
Wood's Green. *E Sus* 2A **38**
Woodside. *Brac* 1B **24**
Woodside. *Herts* 1A **18**
Woodstock. *Oxon* 3A **4**
Wood Street Village. *Surr* 3B **24**
Woolage Green. *Kent* 1C **41**
Woolage Village. *Kent* 3C **31**
Woolbeding. *W Sus* 3A **34**
Woolhampton. *W Ber* 2B **22**
Woolmer Green. *Herts* 3A **8**
Woolston. *Sotn* 1A **42**
Woolton Hill. *Hants* 2A **22**
Woolverstone. *Suff* 1B **12**
Woolwich. *G Lon* 1C **27**
Wootton. *IOW* 3B **42**
Wootton. *Kent* 1C **41**
Wootton. *Oxon* 1A **14**
   (nr. Abingdon)
Wootton. *Oxon* 3A **4**
   (nr. Woodstock)

Wootton Bridge. *IOW* 3B **42**
Wootton Common. *IOW* 3B **42**
Wootton St Lawrence. *Hants* 3B **22**
Worcester Park. *G Lon* 2A **26**
Workhouse Green. *Suff* 1D **11**
Worlds End. *Hants* 1C **43**
World's End. *W Ber* 1A **22**
World's End. *W Sus* 1B **46**
Wormingford. *Essx* 1D **11**
Worminghall. *Buck* 1C **15**
Wormley. *Herts* 1B **18**
Wormley. *Surr* 2B **34**
Wormshill. *Kent* 3C **29**
Worplesdon. *Surr* 3B **24**
Worth. *Kent* 3D **31**
Worth. *W Sus* 2B **36**
Worthing. *W Sus* 2D **45**
Worting. *Hants* 3C **23**
Wotton. *Surr* 1D **35**
Wotton Underwood.
   Buck .3C **5**
Wouldham. *Kent* 2B **28**
Wrabness. *Essx* 1B **12**
Wraysbury. *Wind* 1C **25**
Wrecclesham. *Surr* 1A **34**
Wright's Green. *Essx* 3D **9**
Writtle. *Essx* 1A **20**
Wrotham. *Kent* 3A **28**
Wrotham Heath. *Kent* 3A **28**
Wroxton. *Oxon* 1A **4**
Wyatt's Green. *Essx* 2D **19**
Wych Cross. *E Sus* 2C **37**
Wyck. *Hants* 2D **33**
Wycombe Marsh.
   Buck 2A **16**
Wyddial. *Herts* 1B **8**
Wye. *Kent* 1A **40**
Wyfold Grange. *Oxon* 3C **15**
Wyke. *Surr* 3B **24**
Wymering. *Port* 2C **43**
Wytham. *Oxon* 1A **14**

Y

Yalding. *Kent* 3A **28**
Yapton. *W Sus* 2B **44**
Yarmouth. *IOW* 3A **42**
Yarnton. *Oxon* 3A **4**
Yateley. *Hants* 2A **24**
Yattendon. *W Ber* 1B **22**
Yeading. *G Lon* 3D **17**
Yelford. *Oxon* 1A **14**
Yelsted. *Kent* 2C **29**
Yiewsley. *G Lon* 3C **17**
Yorkletts. *Kent* 2A **30**
Young's End. *Essx* 3B **10**

SAFETY CAMERA INFORMATION

PocketGPSWorld.com's CamerAlert is a self-contained speed and red light camera warning system for SatNavs and Android or Apple iOS smartphones/tablets. Visit www.cameralert.co.uk to download.

Safety camera locations are publicised by the Safer Roads Partnership which operates them in order to encourage drivers to comply with speed limits at these sites. It is the driver's absolute responsibility to be aware of and to adhere to speed limits at all times.

By showing this safety camera information it is the intention of Geographers' A-Z Map Company Ltd., to encourage safe driving and greater awareness of speed limits and vehicle speed. Data accurate at time of printing.